Leadership Map

Leadership Map
The Secret to Inspiring and Motivate Teams

Fábio Correa Xavier

Copyright © 2024 Fábio Correa Xavier
All rights reserved.

No part of this book may be reproduced or stored in a retrieval system, or transmitted in any form or by any means, electronic, mechanical, photocopying, recording, or otherwise, without express written permission of the publisher.

ISBN: 9798302206763
Publishing imprint: Independently published.

I dedicate this book with all my love and gratitude to those who are the real reason for my journey:

To my wife, Andressa Carvalho, for being my rock, my unconditional support and my inexhaustible source of love and inspiration. Your strength and affection motivate me to be a better man and leader every day.

To my children, Gabriel and Isabella, who are my greatest pride and hope for the future. May you always follow your dreams with courage and determination, knowing that success comes with effort and integrity.

And to my mother, Ana Maria, who from the beginning taught me the values that I carry with me to this day. His wisdom, example, and love formed the basis of all that I am.

This book is for you, who give me reasons to continue and always seek the best.

With regard to commitment, commitment, effort, dedication, there is no middle ground. Either you do something well or you don't.

- Ayrton Senna (from Brazil!)

Foreword

I'm from Minas Gerais, from Belo Horizonte. The similarities began right at the beginning of the book. I know well how Fábio's values guided him to a journey as spectacular and dynamic as the one in this book. Mineiro is a mixture of gold and earth, silence and bravery. This book is no different. Between one coffee and another, at a big event, we drew up the first plan for me to be here with you today. Fábio made me think: what is on the leadership map?

When we think of leadership, we are often led to imagine iconic figures, those who seem to have been born to lead, endowed with unshakable confidence and a clear vision. However, the true essence of leadership lies not in titles or an aura of perfection, but rather in the ability to inspire and motivate those around us to reach their full potential. It's about creating an environment where each individual feels valued and part of something bigger than themselves.

Fábio Correa Xavier, in his book *Mapa da Liderança (Map of Leadership)*, invites us to explore this journey of authentic and meaningful leadership. He reminds us that leadership is a choice, not a position. It is a daily practice of living our values and committing to integrity and perseverance. Throughout the pages of this book, Fábio shares his personal and professional experiences, offering valuable insights into how to lead with purpose and passion.

What makes this book truly special is Fábio's approach to demystifying the concept of the perfect leader. It encourages us to embrace our imperfections, to see our flaws not as weaknesses but as opportunities for growth and connection. In doing so, he shows us that vulnerability is a powerful force in building trust and mutual respect within teams.

Fábio also highlights the importance of a clear and inspiring vision, which serves as a compass for innovation and job satisfaction. He reminds us that passion is the fuel that drives both leaders and their teams to overcome challenges and achieve excellence. And, perhaps most importantly, it teaches us that effective communication and empathy are key to creating a collaborative and engaged environment.

Empathy and engagement are topics that he addresses in depth, highlighting that empathy is not just an emotional skill, but a strategic pillar that strengthens leadership. It reflects on how understanding and valuing everyone's perspectives can foster a more collaborative and engaged environment. This ability to genuinely connect with others is what sets leaders apart who inspire in lasting ways.

The World Health Organization estimates that, globally, companies lose US$ 1 trillion dollars per year in lost productivity due to the mental health of their employees. But this loss of profit goes beyond absenteeism and has significant consequences in all areas of companies.

One of the largest organizational consulting firms in the world, Gallup, published in the Harvard Business Review an analysis aggregating decades of data collected on variables that lead to positive results for both companies and employees. And the main variable they identified was the level of engagement with the work.

This survey shows that having a high level of engagement helps companies to have greater productivity with their teams, higher quality products, and greater profitability. But there is a clear problem that emerges in this situation: anxious and stressed people cannot have high engagement with their work.

After all, if a professional cannot express his ideas because he is afraid of being judged, how will this person do his best in this environment? In addition, research published in the journal Cogent Business & Management reveals that low levels of engagement lead to decreased morale and productivity of teams, increased turnover, higher rates of workplace accidents and large financial losses for companies – which could be avoided.

On the other hand, satisfied and engaged employees report 74% less stress, 106% more energy at work, 50% higher productivity, 13% fewer sick days, 29% more satisfaction with their lives, and 40% less likely to have burnout. In general, professionals engaged with their work are 85% more efficient in their tasks and 300% more innovative in the solutions generated.

These data are the result of the research of Paul Zak, an American neuroeconomist who developed pioneering research in this area, studying biology, psychology and neuroscience to better understand the biological part of our decision-making. Their findings show that trust is not just an abstract concept, but a biological function that can be measured and stimulated.

Creating a culture of trust within companies can break toxic cycles of suffering and create a workspace that protects everyone's mental health. This is the main difference between companies in which employees are engaged and participative, and organizations in which people do not feel good in the work environment.

This is also crucial when we consider that, according to WHO data, Brazil is the most anxious country in the world.

In companies that foster a culture of trust, employees collaborate better with each other, stay longer in their positions, have lower stress levels, and report being happier in their lives as a whole, not just at work. But the reason behind this is no magic; it is our biology.

Both in our personal lives and in the professional sphere, we choose people to interact with through trust, which is the basis of human relationships. This is called reliability biology.

Our brain is a complex machine that not only receives and processes information, but also profoundly influences the way we interact with each other. Research in neuroscience shows that oxytocin is an essential neurotransmitter that modulates our relationship with other people – more specifically, oxytocin is related to the way we trust each other. This neurotransmitter is released in our body when we have positive social connections.

In times of adversity, having good relationships becomes crucial. Fábio guides us through strategies to lead in turbulent times and emerge stronger. It also shows us how dynamic delegation can relieve the leader of daily tasks, empower and develop team members.

Leadership Map is more than a book; it's an invitation to embark on a journey of self-discovery and continuous development. Fábio inspires us to lead with courage, integrity, and a clear vision, leaving a positive impact on the people and organizations we touch.

As you read this book, I hope you feel motivated to lead with a higher purpose, to inspire those around you, and to contribute to a future where leadership is synonymous with inspiration, transformation, and genuine care. Together, we can shape a world of regenerative leaders, so that each individual feels valued and part of something truly meaningful.

With admiration,

Flávia Lippi

Founder of IDHL and Specialist in Neurobehavior

Coord. Innovation Observatory of the Future of Work (OFC) at PUC SP

Summary

- My Journey 12
- Demystifying the Perfect Leader 18
- Vision with Purpose 34
- Passion in Action 55
- Integrity 73
- The Art of Communication in Leadership 86
- Empathy and Engagement 100
- Decision and Direction 112
- Continued Growth 123
- Resilience and Recovery 134
- Dynamic Delegation 148
- Innovation and Inspiration 162
- Words convince, example drags! 179
- About The Author 192
- Books and chapters by the author 196

MY JOURNEY

On a rainy morning in June, in a barracks in Juiz de Fora, the commander called me for a mission. I was 21 years old and a lieutenant in the Army, recently graduated, full of ambitions and expectations. My task? Leading a group of soldiers in a complex operation, which would require not only technical knowledge, but courage and, above all, confidence in myself and the team.

In that moment, I realized something crucial: leadership is never about you. It's not about how strong, smart, or capable you are on your own. Leadership is about the ability to inspire, to move a team to act towards a common goal, even in the most uncertain moments.

This first experience as a leader deeply marked my trajectory and is the foundation of what I share in this book. Over the years, I've had the opportunity to lead in challenging environments – from military operations to digital transformation projects in large public organizations. What I learned, however, is that the essence of leadership does not change, regardless of the scenario: leaders inspire, influence, and guide based on solid values.

The concept of leadership is often mystified as something reserved for those who occupy prestigious positions, those who master the art of oratory or who were born with some special "gift". But this view is limited and, dare I say, mistaken. True leadership is in daily actions, in small gestures of integrity, in the ability to listen more than talk, to serve more than command. And most of all, leadership is in recognizing that you'll never be perfect — and that's okay.

Throughout this book, I want to take you, the reader, on a journey that mixes practical experiences, lessons learned and personal stories, not so that you can see what I have done or who I am, but so that you can find in my stories reflections of your own ability to lead. This is not a theory book, nor a technical manual. It's an honest conversation about what it means to lead authentically, and how that can be cultivated in anyone who is willing to learn.

Leading, for me, has always been a balancing act: between pragmatism and inspiration, between knowing how to delegate and, at the same time, rolling up your sleeves and doing what is necessary. During my career, in times of crisis and transformation, I often asked myself, "What should I do now?" And the answer, invariably, boiled down to a simple truth: show by example.

You can inspire people with your words, but it's by your actions that they'll truly believe you. I learned this over years leading projects in high-pressure scenarios. I learned this in emotional and professional battles, in which the choices were not easy and the paths were not always clear.

One of the most eye-opening moments of my life was when, as CIO, I had to lead a digital transformation process in an environment traditionally averse to change. There was resistance, skepticism, and, to be honest, days when I myself doubted whether it was possible to transform the organization's mindset. However, one thing has kept me steadfast: the belief that leading with integrity and clarity of purpose always makes a difference.

In difficult meetings, as I faced resistance from those who feared change, I kept one premise in mind: To lead, you first need to earn the trust of those who follow you. And trust is not earned with empty promises or grand speeches – it is built with consistency. In those moments, I took a simple approach: I listened more than I spoke, I understood the concerns, but I made it clear that change was inevitable—and that we all had a role to play in making it successful.

It is this philosophy that permeates every page of this book. I want you to see that leadership is not about being perfect or unbeatable. Rather, it's about being human. It's about connecting with people on a deep level, understanding their motivations and fears, and helping them see what's possible. Leading is an invitation to get out of your comfort zone, and that's exactly what I'm proposing here: that you, like me, accept the challenge of being a better leader every day.

But understand, this does not mean that the path will be easy. There will be failures. There will be times when you question everything. And that's okay. Every mistake, every stumble, is part of the journey. What matters is how you get up and, even more, how you help others get up too.

One of my greatest inspirations has always been the motto I learned in the Armed Forces: "Words convince, but example drags." I've lived this motto at every stage of my career, whether as a professor, CIO, or board member. Leading by example is what creates impact, it is what transforms.

Leadership Map is a collection of the experiences and insights I've accumulated over the years, each chapter dedicated to a vital aspect of leadership:

Chapter 1: Demystifying the Perfect Leader

In this chapter, we challenge the idea of the perfect leader, exploring how authenticity and vulnerability are essential for effective leadership. Rather than striving for perfection, leaders should embrace their imperfections and use them as tools to build connections and trust with their teams. True leadership comes from the courage to be human.

Chapter 2: Vision with Purpose

Leadership starts with a clear vision and purpose that inspires others. This chapter explores how to develop a vision that goes beyond short-term goals and creates a sense of mission within teams. Here, the focus is on leading with purpose, ensuring that every action and decision is aligned with deep and meaningful values.

Chapter 3: Passion in Action

Passion is the engine that drives transformative leadership. In this chapter, we discuss how passion for work and goals not only motivates the leader, but also energizes and inspires the team. Passion makes a leader resilient and determined to face obstacles with courage and determination.

Chapter 4: Integrity

Integrity is the foundation of lasting leadership. Leading with integrity means being true to your values and to what you promise. This chapter covers how consistency between words and actions builds trust, a key element for any leader who wants to have a positive and lasting impact on their organization.

Chapter 5: The Art of Communication in Leadership

Effective communication is the heart of leadership. Here, you'll learn the importance of clear, empathetic, and strategic communication to align and motivate your team. The chapter highlights how leaders who master the art of listening and communicating assertively are able to create collaborative and inspiring environments.

Chapter 6: Empathy and Engagement

Empathy-based leadership creates deeper connections and a work environment where people feel valued. This chapter explores how empathy can be a powerful tool for increasing engagement, improving performance, and fostering a sense of belonging within the team.

Chapter 7: Decision and Direction

Making clear and firm decisions is a core skill for a leader. This chapter looks at the decision-making process at critical moments and how to stay on track, even in situations of uncertainty. Leadership requires courage to make difficult decisions, balancing reason with intuition.

Chapter 8: Continued Growth

Leadership is a constant learning process. In this chapter, we explore the importance of personal and professional growth for leaders who want to continue inspiring their teams. Continuous learning is key to innovation and adaptation in an ever-changing world.

Chapter 9: Resilience and Recovery

Moments of crisis test the true strength of a leader. This chapter delves into the importance of resilience and how the ability to bounce back from adversity shapes leaders who are able to face difficult times with determination and serenity, inspiring their teams to do the same.

Chapter 10: Dynamic Delegation

Delegating is not just a matter of efficiency, but of developing trust and autonomy within teams. This chapter discusses how effective delegation is a tool for empowering team members, allowing leaders to focus on what's essential while their teams grow and take on more responsibility.

Chapter 11: Innovation and Inspiration

Visionary leaders know that innovation is the path to lasting success. In this chapter, we discuss how leaders can foster a culture of innovation and inspiration, where teams feel free to experiment and create. The ability to innovate is what distinguishes leaders who transform their organizations and industries.

Chapter 12: Words Convince, Example Drags!

Leading by example is the fundamental principle that permeates the entire book. In this final chapter, we reinforce that actions speak louder than words and that a leader's legacy is defined by the impact of their actions on people's daily lives and the organization's culture. Example is the greatest leadership tool.

Leadership Map is more than a book; it's an invitation to embark on a journey of self-discovery and growth. My wish is that this guide inspires you to lead with courage, integrity, and a clear vision, leaving a legacy to the people and organizations you touch.

I believe that the future belongs to leaders who can balance innovation with empathy, who have the courage to make difficult decisions, but also the humility to listen and learn from others. This book doesn't offer ready-made answers, but it does give you tools to find your own answers, so you can walk your path as a leader, with courage and purpose. Together, we can shape a future where leadership is synonymous with inspiration, transformation, and genuine care.

Fábio Correa Xavier

1

DEMYSTIFYING THE PERFECT LEADER

There is nothing more powerful than allowing others to see your vulnerability. It is from this openness that true connection and leadership emerge.
— Brené Brown

Before we talk about *Inspiring Leadership*, it is important to demystify the idea of the perfect leader. There is no perfect leader. The leader, no matter how good he is, makes mistakes. The search for perfection in leadership is a trap that many fall into, but few manage to get out of. The idea of the impeccable leader, always in control and unwavering in the face of any adversity, is a myth that is linked to unrealistic expectations and not to the practice of leadership. So, before we address some fundamental characteristics for an inspiring leader, let's deconstruct, in this chapter, the search for the perfect leader, highlighting how vulnerability and authenticity are not only human, but also essential for effective and inspiring leadership.

On the journey to demystify the perfect leader, it is critical to recognize that vulnerability not only humanizes the leader but also serves as a foundation for truly inspiring and effective leadership. Drawing inspiration from Brené Brown's reflections, especially her book "The Courage to Be Imperfect," we realize that the connection between vulnerability and leadership is deep and transformative.

Contrary to the common belief that vulnerability is synonymous with weakness, it is actually a testament to courage and authenticity. Leaders who allow themselves to be vulnerable, who openly admit their faults and fears, create a work environment based on trust and collaboration. That's because vulnerability makes us genuinely human and close, establishing common ground that encourages others to open up and connect in meaningful ways.

By sharing their own vulnerabilities, inspirational leaders dismantle the illusion of perfectionism and foster a culture where transparency reigns. This approach invites teams to share their experiences and challenges, creating a space where free expression is valued, and ideas can flow freely. Such an environment not only facilitates open and honest communication but also sees mistakes as fundamental to the learning and growth process.

In this context, innovation emerges as a natural byproduct of vulnerability. An environment that embraces error as an integral part of development encourages experimentation and creativity. Leading with vulnerability means creating a safe space for calculated risks, in which innovation is not only possible, but strongly encouraged. This fosters a culture of curiosity and exploration, in which new ideas are celebrated, and creativity can thrive.

Additionally, being transparent about difficulties not only demonstrates the ability to face adversity with integrity but also inspires the team to develop their own resilience. This honesty fosters a mindset where obstacles are seen as opportunities for innovation and growth, modeling a proactive approach to overcoming challenges.

At the same time, authenticity is consolidated as a vital foun-

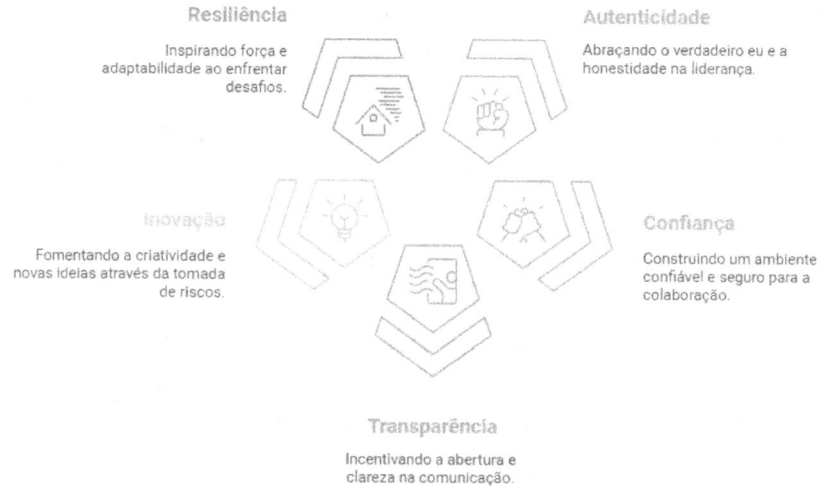

dation for truly genuine leadership. Bill George, in "True North: Discover Your Authentic Leadership," illustrates that being authentic entails leading anchored in deep values, principles, and beliefs, even if it exposes vulnerabilities. Authentic leaders reject the false mask of perfection, opting instead for a transparency that humbly reveals their flaws and limitations. This honesty not only keeps them aligned with their "true north" but also ultimately guides them in their decisions and actions, ensuring that they stay true to themselves and their core values.

The narrative of the perfect leader, often idealized, contrasts sharply with the reality of our human condition, full of flaws and imperfections. Authenticity, by allowing us to embrace our integral humanity, creates bridges of genuine connection with our teams. It teaches us that the essence of leadership lies not in the absence of failures, but in the ability to be true to oneself and others, thus inspiring authentic confidence.

This authentic approach to leadership not only inspires faith but also fosters an environment in which innovation, engagement, and loyalty flourish. When leaders demonstrate openness and vulnerability, they instill in their team members a sense of psychological safety. This means that people feel safe expressing their ideas, sharing their concerns, and even admitting their mistakes without fear of reprisals. This environment of psychological safety is critical for the development of highly effective and innovative teams.

In addition, leaders who practice authenticity promote a leadership model that values self-knowledge and personal growth. By recognizing and acknowledging their own development needs, they encourage a climate of continuous learning and constant improvement. This attitude establishes an organizational culture in which personal development is seen as an integral part of collective success.

Ultimately, leading with authenticity and vulnerability is an invitation for everyone in the organization to be more human, more connected, and more engaged. This form of leadership not only boosts morale and job satisfaction but also drives performance and effectiveness. Authentic leaders, by staying true to their "true north", not only achieve their goals, but also inspire their teams to reach their full potential, creating a truly inspiring and transformative leadership legacy.

Simon Sinek, in his book "Leaders Serve Last," challenges the conventional idea of the perfect leader by arguing that true leadership requires an altruism that puts the needs of others above one's own. Sinek introduces us to the conception that mistakes and failures, far from being signs of weakness, are essential components of growth and innovation within a team. It introduces the concept of the "circle of safety," a support structure that leaders must create around their teams, in which vulnerability is accepted and even encouraged. This safe environment fosters a space where everyone feels comfortable being their authentic selves, sharing their concerns, and most importantly, their mistakes.

An example of this is Satya Nadella's leadership at Microsoft. Since Satya Nadella took on the role of CEO of Microsoft in 2014, he has not only revitalized the company's image, but also instigated an internal cultural revolution, replacing the old "culture of knowledge" with a "culture of learning." This transformation is a testament to Nadella's authentic and adaptive leadership, which focuses on innovation and continuous growth for both the organization and its employees. In his book "*Hit Refresh: The Quest to Rediscover Microsoft's Soul and Imagine a Better Future*", Nadella discusses this journey of transformation. He chronicles how, under his leadership, Microsoft embraced change, encouraging a mindset where learning from mistakes is seen not as a failure, but as a crucial step in the innovation process. Not only does this book offer *insights* into Nadella's vision for the company, but it also serves as a guide for any leader who aspires to cultivate a resilient and adaptable work environment. By fostering an environment where questioning and the pursuit of knowledge are valued over mere possession of information, Nadella has been able to inspire a new era of creativity and innovation at Microsoft.

Additionally, through interviews and speeches, Nadella constantly emphasizes the importance of a culture that values learning, diversity, and inclusion. These communications reinforce their belief that for an organization to thrive in an ever-changing global marketplace, it must not only adapt to new technologies but also cultivate a workforce that reflects the diversity of its global users.

And this philosophy is not just in speech, it was used, for example, in the way Microsoft approached the development of Azure, its cloud computing platform. Under Nadella's leadership, the Azure team was encouraged to experiment and learn from each project, resulting in a series of innovations that cemented Microsoft's position as a leader in cloud services. This success was not the result of rigidly following established plans, but rather of a flexible and adaptive approach to product development, a hallmark of the Nadella era.

Nadella's leadership at Microsoft vividly illustrates how vulnerability, authenticity, and a willingness to learn from mistakes can transform an organization. By replacing the "culture of knowledge" with a "culture of learning," Nadella not only redefined success at Microsoft, but also established a new paradigm for leadership in the twenty-first century.

Authenticity and vulnerability emerge as essential foundations in building leadership that is both accessible and deeply human. This approach deconstructs the archaic notion of leaders as distant and infallible figures and replaces it with an image of leadership rooted in empathy, understanding, and the ability to truly connect with others. It is a form of leadership that not only brings leaders and followers closer together, but also inspires genuine trust and loyalty, grounded in authenticity and openness.

An emblematic example of this authentic and vulnerable leadership is Jacinda Ardern, Prime Minister of New Zealand during the 2020 pandemic. His tenure during the COVID-19 crisis has remarkably illustrated how powerful vulnerability and authenticity can be in leading a country against a backdrop of calamity and uncertainty. Ardern did not hesitate to show her own concerns and compassion at critical moments, communicating with the audience in an open and sincere manner. She emphasized community- and science-based decisions, standing firm in her policies to protect the health and well-being of New Zealand citizens, all while sharing the struggles and challenges facing the government.

His ability to lead with vulnerability, expressing genuine emotions in times of crisis, has not diminished his authority, but on the contrary, has amplified the public's trust in his leadership. Ardern demonstrated that it is possible to be a strong and decisive leader while being open and vulnerable. This approach humanized the leadership figure, showing that the ability to feel and express compassion is not a weakness, but a strength that can bring people together, especially in times of adversity. By embedding vulnerability and authenticity into her leadership, Ardern has been able to not only guide her country through one of the biggest global crises of the century, but also strengthen New Zealand's social fabric, fostering a sense of unity and solidarity among New Zealanders. She highlighted the importance of caring for each other and the community, values that have deeply resonated both nationally and internationally.

We can see that leading with authenticity and vulnerability is a testament to leadership that recognizes the strength in humanity and genuine connection. Leaders like Ardern exemplify how transparency, empathy, and compassion not only boost morale and foster collective resilience but also redefine what it means to be an effective leader in the contemporary world. They show us that true leadership is about building bridges, not walls; about opening, not closing; and, more importantly, about being true to yourself and the values that guide your actions.

By embracing vulnerability and authenticity, leaders foster a culture where the fear of failure is replaced by the courage to innovate. This not only increases creativity, but also encourages a continuous learning environment, where adapting to change becomes an integral part of the organizational culture. This environment fosters not only individual growth but also strengthens the resilience of the team.

In addition to examples of leadership that embody authenticity and vulnerability, there are valuable lessons to be learned from leaders who have faced significant failures, learned from their mistakes, and emerged stronger and more effective. These cases highlight the importance of resilience and the ability to overcome, which are fundamental for Inspiring and transformative Leadership.

Howard Schultz's tenure at Starbucks is a fascinating case about resilience in leadership and the importance of staying true to an organization's core values, even in the face of breakneck success or the most daunting challenges. Schultz, in recognizing that his own decisions had inadvertently pushed Starbucks out of its core, demonstrated a rare quality of leadership: the capacity for critical self-evaluation followed by decisive corrective action.

The crisis period in 2008 was a turning point for both Schultz and Starbucks. After a rapid global expansion, the company found itself during a sharp decline in performance, exacerbated by the global economic crisis. At this critical juncture, Schultz made the decision to return as CEO of the company, a position he had left in 2000. This return was not only symbolic, but also a palpable commitment to Starbucks' revitalization.

In "Onward: How Starbucks Fought for Its Life without Losing Its Soul," Schultz describes in detail how he guided the company back to its original principles, focusing on quality, sustainability, and social responsibility. He implemented significant changes, from renovating stores to revamping the customer experience, always with the goal of reigniting the passion for coffee excellence and human connection that had defined Starbucks since its founding.

Schultz's open acknowledgment of his mistakes and his willingness to change course not only saved Starbucks from financial ruin but also cultivated a stronger, more cohesive company culture. This transparency reinforced employee loyalty and respect, who felt more connected to a company that valued honesty and integrity over short-term profit. Additionally, by restoring Starbucks' commitment to its core values, Schultz was able to regain the trust of customers, who realized the company's genuine dedication to delivering not only high-quality products but also making a difference in the community and the environment.

This example resonates deeply with the ideas presented earlier about the importance of authenticity, vulnerability, and resilience in leadership. Schultz not only navigated Starbucks through turbulent times, but he also redefined what it means to be a responsible and visionary leader in the twenty-first century. His legacy at Starbucks serves as a powerful reminder that true leaders are those who face adversity with courage, stay true to their principles, and inspire everyone around them to do the same.

Steve Jobs' trajectory is emblematic not only for the revolutionary impact of his innovations, but also for the lessons of resilience and redemption he offers. His dismissal from Apple in 1985 could have marked the end of his career in technology; instead, it turned into a chapter of introspection and personal growth. During his years away from Apple, Jobs didn't just lament his failure but chose to see this adversity as an opportunity to learn and evolve.

After his departure from Apple, Jobs did not give in to discouragement; rather, he saw this phase as releasing the burden of success, allowing him to start anew. It was during this time that he founded NeXT and Pixar, both companies that would go on to have a substantial impact in their respective fields. NeXT worked on software innovations that would become central to Apple's future, while Pixar revolutionized the world of animation with hits like "Toy Story." More than that, it was during this period of exploration and creation that Jobs met his future wife, Laurene Powell, adding a deeply meaningful personal dimension to his journey of rediscovery.

This period of reflection and learning prepared Jobs for his triumphant return to Apple in 1997, when the company was facing a financial and identity crisis. With a renewed vision and a more mature approach to leadership, Jobs began one of the largest corporate *turnarounds* in history. He simplified the company's product line, focusing on innovation and design, and introduced a series of products that redefined entire categories – the iMac, the iPod, the iPhone and the iPad. Not only did these products save Apple from the brink of bankruptcy, but they also set new standards for the tech industry, profoundly influencing the way we live, work, and communicate.

In his signature speech to Stanford graduates in 2005, Jobs reflected on the importance of moving forward, even when the path seems uncertain. He highlighted the idea that being fired from Apple was the best thing that could have happened to him at that time. The pain of his public separation was replaced with the freedom to be a beginner again, free to enter one of the most creative phases of his life. This period of introspection and new beginnings not only allowed Jobs to recharge his creative batteries but also helped him cultivate a renewed perspective on what it means to lead and innovate.

Jobs' story illustrates the importance of viewing failure not as an end, but as a starting point for growth. Their ability to learn from mistakes, adapt, and apply those learnings to future endeavors is a testament to the power of resilience. Jobs demonstrated that with the right mindset, the most challenging periods can turn into sources of inspiration and innovation. Furthermore, this journey emphasizes the value of persistence and long-term vision in leadership. Even when faced with skepticism and doubt, he remained steadfast in his belief in Apple's potential to change the world.

These leaders exemplify the idea that to err is human and that failure can be a precursor to growth and innovation. Schultz and Jobs showed that rather than allowing mistakes to define their legacy, they can be used as steppingstones to reach new heights of success. Both led with a mixture of humility and determination, acknowledging their flaws and working tirelessly to overcome them. Self-knowledge is constant, daily and permanent. It is a super complex and challenging journey, but essential for anyone who wants to better understand their emotions, thoughts, and behaviors. This practice can transform lives, both personally and professionally.

The true measure of a leader is not found in his ability to avoid mistakes, but in his resilience to face them, learn from them and emerge stronger. By embracing this reality, leaders can inspire their teams to adopt a similar mindset, fostering a culture of continuous learning, adaptability, and innovation. Leadership, then, becomes less about striving for perfection and more about committing to personal and organizational growth.

Thus, challenging the myth of the perfect leader does not mean accepting mediocrity; It is an invitation to recognize and celebrate the complexity and humanity inherent in leadership. By integrating vulnerability, authenticity, and "learning from mistakes" into their practices, leaders can build more united, resilient, and engaged teams, prepared to face challenges with collective trust and determination. In the end, it is shared humanity, with all its imperfections, that can be a leader's greatest strength.

Schematized Summary of the Chapter

1. The Myth of the Perfect Leader

The search for a perfect leader is an illusion. Leaders, like any human being, make mistakes and have vulnerabilities. Authenticity and vulnerability, far from being weaknesses, are qualities that strengthen the connection with the team and promote an environment of trust and innovation.

2. Vulnerability as a Force

- **Humanizes the leader:** Demonstrating vulnerability creates a deeper connection with the team.
- **Fosters trust:** A vulnerable leader inspires confidence because they demonstrate authenticity.
- **Encourages innovation:** A safe environment to make mistakes fosters experimentation and creativity.

- **Strengthens resilience:** Learning from mistakes and overcoming challenges together increases team resilience.

3. Authenticity as a Pillar of Leadership

- **Alignment with values:** Authentic leaders act in accordance with their values, inspiring trust and loyalty.
- **Transparency:** Honesty about your flaws and limitations creates an environment of transparency and open communication.
- **Connection with the team:** Authenticity strengthens the bonds between the leader and the team, fostering a sense of belonging.

4. Examples of Authentic Leaders

- **Satya Nadella:** Transformed Microsoft into a company more focused on culture and innovation, valuing learning and adaptation.
- **Jacinda Ardern:** Demonstrated empathy and vulnerability during the pandemic, strengthening the population's trust in New Zealand.
- **Howard Schultz:** It recognized and corrected Starbucks' mistakes, restoring customer and employee trust.
- **Steve Jobs:** He overcame adversity and became one of the most innovative leaders of his generation, showing that failure can be a steppingstone to success.

5. Benefits of Authentic and Vulnerable Leadership

- **Increased team engagement:** People feel more connected and motivated when they work with an authentic leader.

- **Increased innovation:** A safe environment for making mistakes and experimenting fosters creativity and the generation of new ideas.
- **Improved communication:** Honesty and transparency facilitate open and honest communication.
- **Strengthening organizational culture:** A culture of authenticity and vulnerability fosters a sense of belonging and purpose.

Conclusion

Authentic and transparent leadership is the key to building stronger, more resilient, and innovative teams. By abandoning the pursuit of perfection and embracing their own humanity, leaders can inspire confidence, create a positive work environment, and achieve extraordinary results.

Keys to Success:

- **Be authentic:** Be yourself and don't be afraid to show your vulnerabilities.
- **Build trust:** Create a safe environment where people feel comfortable expressing their ideas and opinions.
- **Encourage innovation:** Value experimentation and learning from mistakes.
- **Communicate clearly:** Be transparent and honest in your communications.
- **Deal with adversity with resilience:** Face challenges with courage and learn from experiences.

By embracing these principles, leaders can create a lasting legacy and inspire others to achieve their own goals.

Keywords: leadership, vulnerability, authenticity, innovation, trust, team, organizational culture.

To reflect

- How can the search for perfection in leadership become a trap? This question leads to reflection on the dangers of idealizing perfection and how it can undermine a leader's effectiveness.

- How can vulnerability be a strength in leadership? This question encourages exploring how vulnerability, rather than being seen as weakness, can strengthen connection and trust within a team.

- What is the role of authenticity in creating a safe and productive work environment? Here, the question focuses on the importance of leading with authenticity and how this contributes to an environment where innovation and open communication are encouraged.

- How can examples of authentic leadership, such as that of Jacinda Ardern and Satya Nadella, inspire leadership practices in your own organization? This question invites the leader to consider how the exemplary practices of other leaders can be applied in his or her context.

- Why is resilience considered an essential component of effective leadership, and how can you cultivate it in your team? The question directs the leader to reflect on the importance of resilience in the face of challenges and how to promote this quality within their team.

Learn more

BROWN, Brené. The courage to be imperfect. Rio de Janeiro: Sextante, 2016.

GEORGE, Bill; SIMS, Peter. True North: Discover Your Authentic Leadership. São Francisco: Jossey-Bass, 2007.

ISAACSON, Walter. Steve Jobs. Simon & Schuster, 2011.

NADELLA, Satya. Hit Refresh: The Quest to Rediscover Microsoft's Soul and Imagine a Better Future. HarperBusiness, 2017.

SCHULTZ, Howard. Onward: How Starbucks Fought for Its Life without Losing Its Soul. Rodale Books, 2011.

SINEK, Simon. Leaders serve themselves last. Rio de Janeiro: Sextante, 2014.

2

VISION WITH PURPOSE

> *Where there is no vision, the people perish; but he that keepeth the law, the same is blessed.*
> *- Proverbius 29:18*

In a fast-paced world, where changes are constant and demands grow at every moment, having a clear vision is not just a differential – it is a necessity. The vision is not only about where you want to go, but also about the "why" you want to get there. It is the beacon that lights the way, even in the darkest nights, and it is the fuel that keeps the flame of passion burning, even in the most challenging times.

In this chapter, we delve into the essence of Inspirational Leadership, which is grounded in the art and science of forging purposeful vision. Imagine yourself as the captain of a ship on the high seas, braving storms and seeking unknown horizons. You're not just the guide: you're the beacon of inspiration for your crew, who rely on you to lead them through uncertainty. What keeps them aligned and dedicated to the journey is not just the promise of lands to be discovered, but the inspiring vision you project – – a compass that points not only to a destination but to a greater purpose, echoing in the heart of each team member and transcending sailing goals to embrace discovery and conquering new worlds.

Building this inspiring vision requires a deep understanding of the "why" of your journey. Simon Sinek, in "Start with the Why", teaches us that the most impactful leaders are those who are clear about the purpose behind their actions. The "Why" is not just a business goal, but a deeper purpose that can inspire and mobilize teams and customers. In *Built to Last*, James Collins and Jerry Porras expand on this idea by showing that the longevity and success of organizations are closely linked to the ability to inspire and mobilize through a clear purpose and a shared vision.

A vision with purpose is more than a goal to be achieved; It's a cause worth fighting for. It should be ambitious to motivate, but tangible enough not to feel unattainable. This view serves as a beacon that lights the way even in the densest fog, ensuring that everyone knows where they are going and why it matters to get there. Purpose gives the soul to vision, transforming objectives into missions, and daily work into a contribution to something greater than oneself.

Communicating this vision effectively is crucial. It should resonate with each person, regardless of their role, inspiring passion and commitment. Inspirational leaders use stories and personal examples to make the vision palpable, allowing team members to see how they contribute to this larger journey. It is essential that this vision is lived daily, reflected in every decision and action, demonstrating that it is not just an ideal, but a constant practice.

However, the path to realizing a vision with purpose is fraught with challenges. Changes in scenery, unexpected obstacles, and doubts can test faith in the vision. Inspirational leaders are adaptable, able to navigate these storms without losing sight of the fundamental purpose. They see challenges as opportunities to strengthen commitment to the vision by adjusting strategies without deviating from the course set by the purpose.

Steve Jobs' story emblematically illustrates how a vision with purpose can not only transform a company but also redefine entire industries. His vision of "putting a personal computer on every person's desk" was not just based on a business goal, but on a deeper purpose of democratizing technology and fostering individual creativity. Jobs was not content with achieving financial goals; It sought to change the way people interacted with technology, making it accessible, intuitive, and an extension of human expression. This clear vision and deep purpose have not only catapulted Apple to success but have also inspired a culture of innovation and design that continues to influence technology, art, and education. Under Jobs' leadership, Apple not only achieved impressive financial goals, but also created world-changing products such as the iPhone, iPad, and Macintosh, each reflecting his vision of making technology personal and revolutionary. This example highlights the power of leadership that combines an ambitious vision with meaningful purpose, leaving a legacy that goes beyond numbers and shapes the future.

But what does it really mean to have a vision with purpose? It is more than a goal or a plan of action. It's an internal compass that guides your decisions, your actions, and most crucially, gives meaning to your team's work. When you lead with a vision that is fueled by genuine purpose, you **create an echo of**

motivation and inspiration that resonates through every level of the organization.

Let's dive a little deeper. How do you develop this vision with purpose? Start by looking within. What are your core values? What makes you get out of bed every morning? These questions may seem simple, but they require deep and honest reflection. Your vision should be an authentic reflection of who you are and what you value. It must align with the beliefs and values of those you lead.

However, having a vision is only part of the challenge. The other equally important aspect is to communicate it effectively. Here, the lessons of *Built to Last* are invaluable. The book highlights that the most powerful visions are those that are lived, not just spoken. It means incorporating that vision into every aspect of your behavior and decisions. When your team sees you living your vision day in and day out, it becomes contagious. They begin to see how their own actions contribute to this larger narrative. But communicating your vision goes beyond personal example. It involves ongoing dialogue, feedback, and most importantly, listening. As a leader, you should be open to hearing how your team perceives and interprets the vision. This two-way interaction not only strengthens the vision but also makes it more inclusive and adaptable to changing circumstances or team goals.

A key aspect of purposeful vision is how it motivates and directs the team. Motivation comes from feeling that the work has meaning, that it is contributing to something bigger. When the team understands and identifies with the vision, they are naturally motivated to do their best. They see each challenge not as an obstacle, but as an opportunity to move towards a common goal.

Inspiring leadership with a purposeful vision also faces its challenges. For example, how do you keep that vision alive and vibrant over time, especially when facing obstacles or turbulence? The keys here are **resilience and adaptability**. A vision with purpose is not a set of rigid instructions, but rather a flexible beacon that can adjust to changes without losing its essence. An example of inspiring leadership, resilience, and adaptability to maintain a purposeful vision, even in the face of significant obstacles, is the trajectory of Yvon Chouinard, founder of Patagonia. The company, known for its unwavering commitment to sustainability and environmental responsibility, has faced several crises and challenges over the years, from environmental issues to changes in the market.

Chouinard details his business philosophy and the journey of his company, Patagonia, in his book "Let My People Go Surfing: The Education of a Reluctant Businessman." In this book, Chouinard shares how Patagonia was founded on principles of minimizing damage to the environment and promoting sustainable practices, a vision he held firm even as the company faced financial and strategic challenges.

One of the most significant crises occurred in the early 1990s, when Patagonia found itself in a difficult financial situation due to rapid expansion. Rather than stray from its core principles, Chouinard saw it as an opportunity to reinforce the company's commitment to sustainability. This led to the implementation of Patagonia's Environmental Responsibility program, which included initiatives such as the use of organic cotton and the launch of the Common Threads program, which encouraged consumers to reduce, reuse, and recycle clothing.

Chouinard's ability to maintain and adapt Patagonia's sustainability vision, even during difficult times, has not only saved the company from financial hardship but also established it as a leader in sustainable business practices. Patagonia's story under Chouinard's leadership is a powerful testament to the impact that purposeful vision, combined with resilience and adaptability, can have on the business world and beyond.

And when we talk about vision with purpose, we cannot ignore the crucial role of values. Leaders with a strong foundation of personal values tend to create visions that reflect those values. This not only ensures the authenticity of the vision but also inspires trust and respect within the team. Team members are naturally attracted to leaders who are genuine and transparent in their intentions and actions. This creates a work environment in which honesty, trust, and integrity flourish.

Going back to Sinek, his concept of "Why" is not just about finding the purpose of your vision, but also about communicating that purpose in a way that resonates with others. That means speaking in the language of emotion and human connection. When you communicate your vision in a way that touches people's hearts and minds, you're not just conveying a message; You are inviting them to be part of a transformative journey.

Let's think about how you can apply these principles in your own leadership journey. Start by reflecting on your current vision. Does it truly reflect your deepest values and purposes? How do you communicate it to your team? Do they feel like they are part of this vision? These questions can help you reevaluate and readjust your approach, ensuring that your leadership is not only effective but also truly inspiring.

At this point, it's important to also consider the impact of your vision on your team or organization's culture. A powerful vision can shape culture in meaningful ways by establishing norms and behaviors that align the team with their shared goals. This is especially important in times of change or crisis, where a clear vision can serve as a point of stability and focus.

Achieving an alignment of your vision with that of your team is not an easy task, but it is incredibly rewarding. A crucial aspect of this alignment is ensuring that each team member understands not only the 'what and how', but especially the 'why' behind their actions. This creates a sense of ownership and responsibility, encouraging everyone to contribute in a meaningful way. When team members see how their work fits into the bigger picture, they are more likely to innovate, take calculated risks, and strive for excellence in their tasks.

Overcoming obstacles is another reality inherent to leadership. Whether you're facing economic challenges, market changes, or internal conflicts, how you sustain and adapt your vision can be decisive. In times of crisis, a vision with purpose acts as an anchor, keeping the team focused and united. It also provides a framework for making tough decisions in a way that is consistent with the values and long-term goals of the team or organization.

In addition, vision profoundly influences organizational culture. A clear and shared vision creates a work environment where innovation is encouraged, communication is open, and **mistakes are seen as learning opportunities**. When culture is aligned with vision, it becomes a powerful catalyst for engagement and achievement of goals. As a leader, it is your responsibility to cultivate this culture by ensuring that it supports and reflects the organization's vision.

However, it is vital to recognize that a vision is not static; It is dynamic and must evolve over time. This does not mean abandoning core values or original purpose but rather adapting them to new realities and opportunities. An evolving vision keeps the organization relevant and responsive, allowing it to thrive in an ever-changing environment.

I emphasize that implementing a vision with purpose is not just about achieving business objectives: it is about creating a legacy. It's about positively impacting people's lives inside and outside the organization. When you lead with a vision that transcends business success and touches on deeper questions of meaning and contribution, you lay the groundwork for lasting impact.

The journey of a leader with a purposeful vision is an ongoing journey of self-discovery, challenges, and growth. It's not just about where you're going, but also about who you become in the process and the impact you have on the people around you. Leadership that uses vision with purpose means navigating uncharted waters, weathering storms, and sometimes readjusting your sails. It is a dynamic and evolving process that requires passion, dedication, and above all, an unwavering belief in your "Why".

The legacy of leadership based on a vision with purpose is measured not only by the results achieved, but also by the difference you make in people's lives. It's about leaving a mark that continues to inspire and influence long after you're gone. As a leader, your greatest triumph is creating an environment in which the vision continues to live and thrive, even in your absence.

In short, a vision with purpose is not a destination, but a compass that guides your daily actions, decisions, and ultimately the trajectory of your leadership. It's about creating something that resonates not only with your personal and professional goals, but also with the values and aspirations of those you lead. By embracing this vision, you not only achieve success but also uplift those around you, creating a legacy of impact and inspiration.

With these principles in mind, I encourage you to reflect on your own leadership journey. What is your vision? Does it reflect a true and deep purpose? How are you communicating this vision to your team and ensuring that it is embedded in every aspect of your organization? Remember, the true measure of your leadership lies in your ability to inspire and motivate others to join you on this journey toward a shared and meaningful future.

Sinek's 'Why'

In a world saturated with information and options, organizations often struggle to differentiate themselves. It is in this context that Simon Sinek, in his 2009 work, offers a revolutionary perspective on how to approach communication and organizational purposes. He posits that, more than ever, it is critical for organizations to connect on a deeper level with their *stakeholders*, not only by showing what they do, but primarily by why they do it.

According to Sinek, many companies have a clear understanding of the "what" they do – that is, the products they make or the services they provide. Some even know "how" they do it, that is, the unique characteristics or processes that make them special. However, there are few who can really articulate "why" they do what they do. And here, we're not talking about profit – that's an outcome. The "Why," as conceptualized by Sinek, refers to the cause, purpose, or belief that gives rise to the organization.

This concept is encapsulated in his model of the "Golden Circle" – three concentric circles, in which the outer circle represents the "What", the middle circle symbolizes the "How" and the core, in turn, represents the "Why". For many companies, communication starts with the outer circle and perhaps reaches the middle, but it rarely touches the core. In contrast, truly inspiring organizations and leaders operate from the inside out; they start with the "Why".

Why is this so crucial? As Sinek aptly argues, "People don't buy *what* you do; they buy the *why* you do." In an era of growing skepticism about corporations, authenticity is valued more than ever. Consumers don't just want one product; They crave a connection, something they can believe in. When an organization can genuinely demonstrate its "Why," she creates that connection.

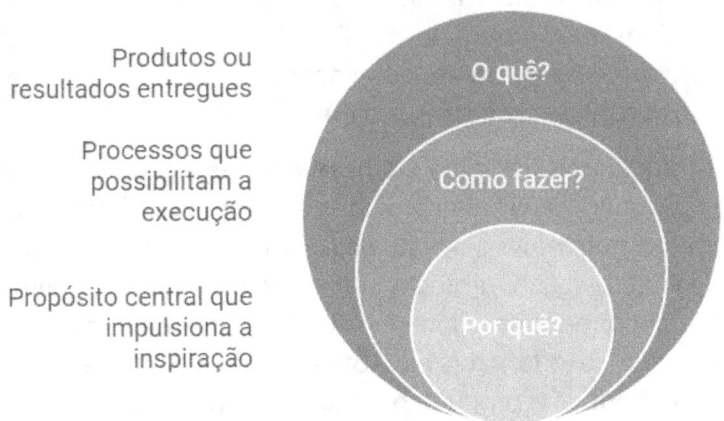

Círculo Dourado de Simon Sinek

Take, for example, Apple. Although it produces computers, phones, and other devices, its "Why" is not about technology per se, but about challenging the *status quo* and thinking differently. This core belief permeates every aspect of your brand and products. As a result, consumers who share this belief are drawn to Apple not only for its products, but for what the company stands for.

Understanding the "Why" doesn't just benefit the relationship with consumers. Internally, a clear understanding of the organization's purpose can guide decision-making, shape culture, and attract talent that aligns with the company's values. Employees aren't just working for a paycheck; They are contributing to a greater cause, something that can be deeply motivating and satisfying.

Sinek's Golden Circle is not just a marketing or communication tool, but a central pillar for building and maintaining resilient and inspiring organizations. In the contemporary world, where trust and authenticity are in high demand, starting with the "Why" is not only desirable but essential. And for those leaders and organizations that embrace and live their "Why," the benefits go beyond financial success, culminating in a lasting and meaningful impact on the world around them.

In addition to tangible success and customer loyalty, a solid and authentic "Why" also provides a competitive differentiator. In saturated markets where multiple companies offer similar products, what really separates a company from the competition is its ability to connect emotionally with its audience. This emotional connection is often forged not through the characteristics or specifications of a product, but rather through the stories, beliefs, and values that a company represents.

Consider iconic brands like Nike. While many companies sell sneakers and sportswear, Nike promotes the idea of overcoming and conquering. His "Why" doesn't focus on selling sneakers, but on the belief that anyone can push their limits and achieve their goals – "*Just Do* It." This powerful mantra resonates on a personal level with many of her clients, creating a deep emotional connection.

This power of "Why" is also evident in marketing and advertising campaigns. Campaigns that encapsulate and clearly express a company's "Why" often resonate more strongly and are more memorable. They don't just focus on selling a product, but on telling a story and sharing a belief or value.

However, it's important to note that while the power of "Why" is undeniable, it also requires consistency and authenticity. Organizations can't just artificially create a "Why" and expect it to resonate. It should be genuine, rooted in the company's culture and history, and reflected in all its actions and decisions. Without this authenticity, *stakeholders* will quickly pick up on the disconnect, and trust will be undermined.

As already discussed, the "Why" of an organization is not – and cannot be – static. As companies grow and evolve, their core purpose may need to be revisited and refined. Leading organizations understand this and engage in regular introspection to ensure that their "Why" remains relevant and true.

For leaders, understanding and communicating the "Why" is an essential skill. Inspirational leaders are those who can clearly articulate the organization's purpose and mobilize their team around that vision. They understand that long-term success is not just based on immediate goals and objectives, but on cultivating a culture that understands, embraces, and lives the "Why" every day. By embracing Sinek's Golden Circle and putting the "Why" at the center of their strategies and communications, organizations not only differentiate themselves in competitive markets, but also cultivate deeper, longer-lasting relationships with customers, employees, and other *stakeholders*, ensuring their legacy in the business landscape.

For the inspirational leader, understanding and articulating the "Why" is crucial, not just as a strategic tool, but as an integral component of their identity and leadership style. Leadership transcends the mere administration or supervision of tasks; it's about shaping visions, instilling passion, and catalyzing action. At its core, Inspirational Leadership is deeply rooted in the ability to connect emotionally and authentically with those you lead.

Every time a leader presents himself in front of his team, he has the opportunity to demonstrate and reinforce the "Why" of the organization. It is this constant reiteration and experience of the purpose that solidifies the organizational culture and creates a sense of cohesion and belonging. In times of uncertainty or adversity, it's the "Why" that serves as a beacon, guiding the team through challenges and keeping them aligned with the bigger picture.

Leaders who neglect the importance of the "Why" often find themselves adrift, with disengaged or misaligned teams. On the other hand, leaders who live and breathe their "Why" not only earn the respect and admiration of their teams, but also inspire action, innovation, and loyalty. They become, in effect, transformational leaders, capable of instigating meaningful change and creating lasting impact.

In the context of Sinek and Golden Circle's insights, the inspirational leader not only understands the importance of the "Why" but also utilizes it as a powerful tool to motivate and inspire. He recognizes that at the end of the day, human beings are not driven solely by logic or tangible benefits; We are emotional beings, seeking purpose, connection, and meaning. By aligning their leadership with these universal principles, the inspirational leader creates an environment in which individuals not only work but also thrive and grow.

While the business world continues to evolve and complexity intensifies, certain principles remain constant. The human need for purpose and connection is one of these immutable principles. For the inspirational leader, understanding and incorporating the "Why" into their approach is not just a strategy; It is a way of life, a fundamental belief that leadership is, above all, an act of service and inspiration. And it's that belief, that authenticity and passion for the "Why," that can differentiate truly great leaders from merely good ones.

The idea behind "Built to Last"

The research of Collins and Porras (1994) highlights the fundamental distinction between firms that simply operate in the market and those that define the market and often redefine their own industries. The concept of "core ideology" that they propose is not just a corporate mission or a vision statement, but a set of core principles that guides all aspects of the organization over time.

The core ideology is the soul of the company. Visionary companies recognize the importance of keeping this core ideology intact and unchanged, regardless of external changes. This does not mean that these companies are resistant to change or innovation. On the contrary, their ability to maintain a solid core is what allows them to be agile and adaptable. While its core ideology remains constant, its approach to achieving its goals – whether through strategies, practices, or operational methods – can and should evolve in response to the ever-changing environment.

This is where the concept of the Golden Circle, proposed by Simon Sinek, comes into play and intertwines with the finds of *Built to Last*. Sinek (2009) highlights three essential components that motivate an organization's actions: the "Why", the "How" and the "What". At the center of this circle, as we have seen, we find the "Why," which resonates strongly with the core ideology proposed by Collins and Porras.

The "Why" refers to the reason why an organization exists, beyond simply generating profit. It is the purpose, the belief, the real reason why the organization was founded. When a company is clear about its "Why", it is able to inspire and mobilize its team, its customers, and even society as a whole. As Sinek often points out,

> *People don't buy what you make; They buy because you do.*

This is the essence of Inspirational Leadership.

Similarly, Collins and Porras realized that visionary companies were motivated not just by profits or market success, but by a deeper ideology, equivalent to Sinek's why. They noted that while products, services, and even industries can change, this core ideology remains constant.

For inspirational leaders, understanding and embodying these concepts is crucial. The ability to articulate and live by the organization's "Why"—its core ideology—is what sets truly transformational leaders apart. They recognize that by centering on a deeper purpose and aligning the organization around that vision, they can achieve a sustainable competitive advantage, cultivate a cohesive corporate culture, and, most importantly, create a lasting legacy.

Both the core ideology proposed by Collins and Porras and Sinek's Golden Circle offer a valuable perspective for leaders and organizations that aspire to more than ephemeral success.

By focusing on their "Why" and staying true to their ideology, organizations not only survive, but thrive regardless of the challenges they face. And it is this set of resilience and ability to inspire that positions them as true visionaries in the business world, with inspiring leaders being the true evangelizers of these concepts.

Vision with purpose

By correlating the *insights* from both books, we realize that a "Vision with Purpose" is crucial to Inspirational Leadership. Leaders must first define and deeply understand the purpose of their actions, the reason why their organization exists. This understanding then serves as the basis for a core ideology, as identified by Collins and Porras (1994), which acts as the foundation upon which the organization is built and evolves.

The combination of Sinek's "Why" clarity and Collins and Porras' core ideology suggests that to effectively inspire, leaders need more than well-crafted strategies or product innovations. They need a purpose and vision that resonates with people, creating deeper connections and inspiring loyalty, innovation, and excellence over time.

In the fast-paced world of business, where change is the only constant, it may seem counterproductive for some organizations to stick to a core principle or purpose. However, the *insights* of Collins, Porras, and Sinek suggest just the opposite. Being anchored in fundamental principles is not an impediment to innovation, but rather a catalyst.

Inspirational leaders understand this nuance. They see the importance of an internal compass not only for themselves but for the entire organization. By staying true to the "Why," they are able to navigate the tumultuous waters of the market, making strategic decisions aligned with the core ideology, even when pressured by short-term demands.

The influence of this type of leadership extends far beyond the walls of the organization. Employees of companies with a strong sense of purpose tend to be more engaged, motivated, and satisfied in their positions. This engagement not only translates into increased productivity, but also into loyalty and retention. In a world where the "war for talent" is increasingly intense, the ability to attract and retain professionals is an invaluable differential.

In addition, customers and *stakeholders* are also influenced by the "Why" of an organization. Contemporary consumers are increasingly interested not only in the products or services they buy, but also in the values and missions of the companies that provide them. Companies that operate with a clear sense of purpose often find a loyal customer base that is willing to support and advocate on their behalf.

In the broader context, society as a whole benefits from companies and leaders who operate with a clear core ideology. Visionary organizations often stand out not only for their success in the marketplace but also for the positive impact they have on their communities and the world at large. Whether using sustainable practices, philanthropic contributions, or breakthrough innovations, companies anchored in a deep "Why" often become forces for good.

In retrospect, what Collins, Porras, and Sinek present to us is not a magic formula, but a profound reminder of the importance of aligning action with purpose. For the inspirational leader, this is not just a business strategy, but a philosophy of life. By embracing and cultivating a core ideology, by understanding and communicating the "Why," leaders have the opportunity not only to build thriving organizations, but to leave an indelible mark on the world, inspiring future generations to do the same.

Schematized Summary of the Chapter

1. Core Concept: Vision with Purpose

- **What it is:** A vision with purpose is a guiding guide that defines an organization's reason for being, in addition to its financial objectives. It is a profound purpose that inspires and motivates everyone involved.

- **Why it matters:** Purposeful vision offers a sense of direction, aligns the team, and differentiates the organization in the marketplace, making it more resilient and impactful.

- **Practical example:** Steve Jobs' vision of "putting a personal computer on every person's desk" has transformed Apple and the tech industry.

2. Key elements

- **Purpose:** The "why" of the organization existing, in addition to profit.

- **Values:** The principles that guide the organization's actions.

- **Goals:** The long-term objectives that the vision seeks to achieve.

- **Communication:** The ability to convey the vision in a clear and inspiring way to the entire team.

3. Implications and Applications

- **Leadership:** Vision with purpose is critical for inspiring leaders, who use vision to guide their teams and make decisions.
- **Organizational culture:** A clear vision shapes the company's culture, creating a more engaged and motivated work environment.
- **Decision-making:** The vision serves as a filter for decisions, ensuring that they are aligned with the organization's purpose.
- **Innovation:** Vision inspires innovation as it directs efforts toward solutions that contribute to the greater purpose.
- **Social impact:** Organizations that have a purposeful vision tend to have a positive impact on society.

4. Conclusion

A vision with purpose is more than a goal; It is a driving force that guides organizations and inspires people. By defining a clear and shared purpose, leaders can build more engaged teams, make more strategic decisions, and create a lasting legacy. Vision with purpose is not just a management tool, but a fundamental element of inspirational leadership.

Keywords: vision, purpose, leadership, organization, values, culture, innovation, social impact.

Call to Action: Leaders, by defining and communicating a clear and inspiring vision, can transform their organizations and create a more meaningful future for all.

To Reflect

- How do you define and communicate the purpose behind your team or organization's vision? This question encourages the leader to reflect on the clarity and effectiveness with which he articulates the "why" that motivates his vision.
- How does your current vision resonate with your team's values and aspirations? This reflection seeks to ensure that the vision is not only personal, but shared and aligned with team members.
- How can you use personal stories and examples to make your vision more inspiring and tangible for your team? This question encourages the leader to think about effective ways to communicate their vision in an engaging and motivating way.
- What strategies do you use to maintain the resilience and adaptability of your vision in the face of challenges and changes? We want to lead the reader to reflect on how the leader can adjust his vision without losing focus on the central purpose.
- How is your vision with purpose shaping organizational culture and motivating your team to achieve excellence? This question encourages the leader to assess the impact of their vision on team culture and overall performance.

Learn more:

COLLINS, James C.; PORRAS, Jerry I. **Built to last**: Successful practices of visionary companies. Rio de Janeiro: Rocco, 1994.

CHOUINARD, Yvon. "**Let My People Go Surfing**: The Education of a Reluctant Businessman." Penguin Books, 2016.Parte superior do formulário

SINEK, Simon. **Start with why**: How great leaders inspire action. São Paulo: LeYa, 2009.

3

PASSION IN ACTION

Passion is energy. Feel the power that comes from focusing on what excites you.
- Oprah Winfrey

Passion is often seen as an inner vigor that drives individuals to pursue their dreams and overcome obstacles. In the context of leadership, this passion becomes the spark that not only lights the way for the leader, but also ignites the spirit of those who follow him. Passion is more than just enthusiasm; It is a deep and persistent force that can turn visions into reality.

Angela Duckworth, in her acclaimed book "Grit: The Power of Passion and Perseverance," delves into the idea that it is not talent, but the combination of passion and perseverance — what she calls "grit" — that are indicative of long-term success. Duckworth points out that passion is not a flash of inspiration, but rather a constant flame that keeps us focused and determined over time.

In a work environment, the presence of a passionate leader has a ripple effect on the team. Passion is contagious. When team members see a leader who is committed, enthusiastic, and truly passionate about what they do, it creates a resonance effect. Employees feel more motivated, engaged, and aligned with the organization's vision.

Duckworth argues that passion doesn't arise from a *eureka* moment of inspiration. Rather, it is a constant flame, a long-term commitment to a goal or activity that is meaningful to us. This sustained passion guides us, keeping us engaged and motivated, even when faced with adversity or seemingly monotonous tasks. It is this persistent passion that fuels our perseverance, allowing us to overcome obstacles and continue on our journey regardless of the difficulties we may encounter.

In the context of visionary and inspiring leadership, the application of "grit" goes beyond personal development and extends to the ability to inspire and motivate teams. Leaders with grit demonstrate an ongoing passion for their vision and an unwavering commitment to their organization's values and goals. They see beyond immediate challenges, focusing on long-term success and accomplishing a larger mission. These leaders serve as beacons of inspiration for their teams, showing that perseverance and dedication are key to turning audacious visions into reality.

A concrete example of this leadership is found in historical figures such as Nelson Mandela. Mandela perfectly exemplifies grit by maintaining his passion for justice and equality, even after decades of incarceration. His perseverance and unwavering belief in his cause inspired not just one nation, but the entire world. Mandela showed that even in the face of extreme adversity, sustained passion and determination can lead to significant and lasting change.

For today's leaders, the lesson is clear: Embodying grit as a leadership principle means passionately committing to your vision and persevering no matter the obstacles. This implies cultivating a mindset that values continuous growth, learning from failure, and resilience in the face of adversity. By demonstrating this persevering passion, leaders can not only achieve their own goals, but also empower their teams to do the same, creating an organizational culture where determination and dedication are valued and rewarded.

Grit is a transformative element in any leader's journey. The combination of passion and perseverance reveals itself as the true indicator of long-term success, both for individuals and organizations. By embracing grit, visionary and inspiring leaders can overcome challenges, achieve lofty goals, and lead their teams to excellence.

Understanding the distinction between true passion and a mere passing excitement is essential in the realm of effective leadership. As clarified by Ryan Holiday in "Ego is the Enemy," genuine passion transcends the superficial form, integrating deeply into the function of our actions and purposes. This concept resonates with Angela Duckworth's observations about how resilience and persistence, fueled by an enduring passion, are vital to achieving long-term goals. Unlike ephemeral excitement, which can falter at the first signs of difficulty, true passion provides the strength needed to overcome obstacles, emanating from a well-defined purpose that guides the leader's actions and strengthens the team's resolve.

Clarity of purpose, as Holiday explains, is key. While passion is often self-centered ("I am passionate about..."), purpose focuses on action and service ("I must do..."). Effective leaders realize that purpose transcends ego, focusing on contributing to something greater than themselves. Not only does this approach lend a clearer and more sustainable direction to passion, but it also helps to communicate the vision more effectively by engaging the team around a shared goal.

Holiday further warns us about how unbridled passion can mask weaknesses, arguing that boundless passion is a poor substitute for discipline, mastery, strength, purpose, and perseverance. In this context, leaders who differentiate their genuine passion from mere emotional impulses are able to shape a cohesive and productive work environment, in which the team deeply understands the "why" of their tasks and is more likely to focus on the "how" and "what" necessary to achieve exceptional results.

Thus, Inspirational Leadership requires more than just dreaming; It requires a passion grounded in clear and realistic purposes. It is the junction of passion with limits—a passion that is consciously driven and constrained by an altruistic purpose. This balance of passion and purpose allows leaders to not only inspire their teams with an engaging vision, but also guide them with a sense of shared mission and accountability. By communicating this purpose authentically and living the values they promote, leaders can create a legacy of lasting impact, leading not just with words, but with the persistent example of their own journey toward achieving ambitious goals. It's authentic passion, rooted in meaningful purpose, that empowers leaders and their teams to overcome adversity, adapt to change, and achieve extraordinary success, creating a lasting legacy of inspiration, innovation, and impact.

However, it is crucial not to confuse this passion with an obsession that blinds sight and judgment. Effective leaders, as Ryan Holiday points out, understand the need to balance passion with a sense of pragmatism and realism. Passion serves as the drive, but it is the discernment and capacity for critical evaluation that drive this impetus, ensuring that both the leader and his team follow a thoughtful and sustainable course. Holiday emphasizes that boundless passion can mask weaknesses, while true strength emerges from passion contained and driven by a clear and realistic purpose.

The energy that passion injects into the work environment has the power to transform not only the operational dynamics, but also the well-being and satisfaction of the team. When individuals engage in projects that spark their passion, work transcends the conventional notion of employment, becoming a true calling. This echoes Holiday's idea that passion should be more than a momentary fervor; It must be guided by a purpose that transcends the ego, focusing on what can be contributed to the world.

Angela Duckworth, when talking about "grit", highlights not only the importance of hard work, but also love for what you do. For truly inspiring leaders, passion is not a mere complement; it is essential, the fuel that sustains their momentum and propels them forward. By leading with this grounded passion, they not only elevate their own performance, but also inspire those around them, building organizations that go beyond basic functioning to flourish and innovate.

The energy that comes from passion in leadership is immeasurable. Leaders who channel their authentic passion effectively become sources of inspiration, motivation, and transformation for their teams. In an ever-evolving corporate landscape, passion—when balanced with perseverance, purpose, and a realistic perspective, as Holiday suggests—becomes essential to achieving true and sustainable excellence. Thus, effective leadership is one that recognizes passion not as an end, but as the means by which a broader and more meaningful impact is sought, both inside and outside the organization.

At the core of Inspirational Leadership, we find a delicate balance between passion and pragmatism. Passion, often seen as the beating heart behind motivation and creative drive, can, in the absence of guidance, become a chaotic force. However, when calibrated and driven by a sense of purpose and realism, it becomes an invaluable tool for leading effectively.

Consider passion not as a wild flame, but as a controlled fire that lights the way forward. This analogy captures the need for leaders to possess not only the energy and enthusiasm that passion brings, but also the wisdom to direct it productively. Like a beacon, passion can guide a team through the darkness of uncertainty, but only if it is contained and focused by a clear purpose. It is this purpose that transforms effervescent passion into a sustainable commitment to long-term goals and objectives.

Take, again, the excellent example of Apple's journey under the leadership of Steve Jobs after his return to the company in 1997. Jobs was notoriously passionate, but it was his ability to align that passion with a clear purpose—to revolutionize personal technology—that allowed Apple to not only survive, but thrive. Jobs demonstrated that true passion in leadership goes beyond enthusiasm for the idea itself; It is a commitment to the realization of this vision that considers the needs and desires of the market and society.

Similarly, the story of Howard Schultz and his reinvention of Starbucks underscores the importance of balancing passion with pragmatism. Schultz didn't hide his passion for coffee and the coffee shop experience. However, his decision to restructure the company and close all stores for a few hours to reskill baristas reflects a pragmatic approach to ensuring that the passion for quality was never compromised by rapid expansion.

Furthermore, Angela Duckworth, in discussing "grit," illustrates that passion, when combined with perseverance, becomes an unstoppable force. In the context of leadership, this means a long-term dedication that persists even in the face of challenges, inspiring teams to do the same. Leaders with "grit" are those who can demonstrate their commitment not just with words, but through consistent actions and a continuous investment in their goals and those of their team.

Therefore, effective leadership requires more than overwhelming passion; It requires the ability to shape that passion with a clear purpose and realistic boundaries. Leaders who master this art not only achieve their own goals, but also cultivate environments where teams are motivated, engaged, and equipped to meet the challenges along the way. In a business world that values speed and innovation, a balanced passion for a strong purpose is key to creating resilient, adaptable, and future-ready organizations.

How passionate leaders transform organizations

In the contemporary business landscape, the presence of truly passionate leaders can transform an organization into a living, pulsating entity whose energy and dedication resonate well beyond the confines of its operations. This fervor in leadership not only inspires and motivates internally, but also shapes the external perception of the organization, establishing it as a renowned brand, recognized for its innovation, quality, and commitment to excellence. This distinction is palpable and creates a magnetism around the organization that attracts customers, partners, and talent, while setting a high bar that challenges competitors.

An example of this dynamic is Tesla, under the leadership of Elon Musk. His passion for innovation in sustainable energy technology has not only revolutionized the auto industry but also turned Tesla into a synonym for innovation and sustainability. Musk exemplifies how a leader's passion can catalyze an organizational culture that prioritizes continuous innovation and the search for solutions that challenge the status quo, moving the entire industry toward a more sustainable future.

In addition, this passion in leadership encourages a growth mindset among employees. When leaders approach each challenge with enthusiasm and relentless determination, they create an environment where fear of failure is minimized, and experimentation and learning are valued. This encourages the team to explore new ideas, embrace innovation, and pursue excellence, knowing that they have the backing and backing of committed leadership. The result is a dynamic organization, in which innovation is not just a goal, but a constant.

Google, known for its innovative and open culture, is another testament to the impact of passion on leadership. The company actively encourages its employees to devote time to personal projects that they are passionate about, resulting in products and services that have shaped the way the world interacts with technology. This commitment to innovation, fueled by the passion of leaders and team members, has established Google as an undisputed leader on multiple technology fronts.

Therefore, at the heart of organizations that not only function, but truly thrive and lead in their industries, we find leaders whose passion transcends the personal and infuses itself into the very essence of the organization. These leaders inspire their teams to push boundaries, innovate relentlessly, and reach levels of excellence that set the standard for everyone else. In an increasingly saturated and competitive business world, genuine passion and commitment to a clear purpose are more than just perks; are the pillars on which lasting success is built.

Embodying Ryan Holiday's perspectives on "Ego is the Enemy," passion in leadership is amplified by authenticity, making it an even more powerful force. Holiday reminds us that passion, when aligned with purpose and limited by reality and self-knowledge, transcends mere excitement or the desire for personal satisfaction. Genuinely passionate leaders, those who don't need to hide behind masks or play roles, radiate an authenticity that establishes fertile ground for trust and mutual respect within the organization. This authenticity, rooted in deep conviction and dedication to something beyond oneself, becomes a valuable currency in a corporate environment often marked by uncertainty and distrust.

For those in leadership positions or aspiring leaders, the journey to cultivating this authentic, purpose-aligned passion begins with introspection. Deeply exploring what really ignites the internal flame and how it aligns with the organization's larger purpose is crucial. This exploration is not an exercise in indulgence, but a process of discovery that grounds leadership in solid and meaningful values. Holiday points out that purpose minimizes the ego, focusing on pursuing something outside of oneself, as opposed to seeking personal pleasure.

True passion in leadership, then, is not just a drive for innovation or a means to overcome challenges; It's a manifestation of authenticity and purpose that shapes thriving organizational cultures. It inspires not only by the intensity of the commitment, but by the genuineness and depth of that commitment. In environments where leadership is driven by such passion, innovation flourishes naturally, challenges are met with resilience, and the collective vision becomes more tangible and achievable.

Angela Duckworth points out that the combination of passion and perseverance, or "grit," distinguishes successful dreamers from those who actually achieve it. When that drive is fueled by authentic passion and a clear purpose, leaders not only achieve their personal goals but also elevate their organizations to new heights. At the heart of successful organizations, we often find leaders whose passion is so evident and contagious that it inspires everyone around them to engage deeply, constantly innovate, and push boundaries, always aspiring to something bigger and more meaningful.

Thus, effective leadership, enriched by authenticity and a well-defined purpose, transcends the limits of ego and self-satisfaction, becoming a powerful catalyst for organizational transformation and the realization of ambitious visions. Leaders who navigate this journey with genuine passion and a sense of purpose not only leave their mark on the organizations they lead, but also shape the future of leadership itself, setting new standards of excellence and inspiration.

The essence of Inspirational Leadership often lies in passion. This is not only a driving force for the individual leader, but the fuel that energizes the entire organization. When a leader genuinely embodies their passion, that authenticity permeates every aspect of the organization, inspiring teams, shaping cultures, and raising standards. The difference between a leadership that simply manages tasks and one that truly inspires lies in this ability to infuse passion into every goal, strategy, and interaction.

Leaders who live their passion don't just catalyze change; They turn visions into fiery missions, infecting everyone around them with a sense of purpose and possibility. This transmission of passion creates an environment in which motivation and engagement are not imposed, but naturally cultivated. These leaders do not lead by authority, but lead by example, demonstrating how passion can transcend obstacles and foster excellence.

Embodying Ryan Holiday's ideas about the importance of aligning passion with purpose, inspiring leaders recognize that true passion is not just a fervor for personal goals, but a dedication to something bigger. They know that authentic passion must be tempered with purpose and realism, creating a dynamic in which aspirations are balanced with awareness of the reality and needs of others. This approach not only enriches the leadership journey, but ensures that passion manifests in ways that benefit the entire organization.

Moreover, these leaders understand, as Angela Duckworth teaches, that perseverance fueled by genuine passion—grit—is essential for long-term success. They apply this drive not only to overcome personal challenges, but also to encourage their teams to embrace and overcome their own difficulties. By doing so, they establish a culture of resilience, creativity, and continuous growth.

Holiday warns us, however, about the risks of a passion unfiltered by wisdom and purpose. He argues that unbridled passion can be counterproductive, masking weaknesses and diverting the focus from what is truly important. Therefore, effective leaders balance their passion with critical reflection, ensuring that their energy not only inspires but also produces tangible, positive results.

By combining Duckworth and Holiday's insights, it is clear that exceptional leaders are those who are driven not only by burning passion, but who also drive that passion with clear purpose and pragmatism. They create organizations where passion inspires excellence, purpose provides direction, and determination overcomes adversity. Such leadership not only achieves great things but also inspires each team member to pursue their own growth and contribute to collective success.

Therefore, the journey to Inspirational Leadership is as much about discovering and nurturing one's own passion as it is about aligning that passion with a greater purpose that transcends the ego. Leaders who master this art not only transform their organizations, but also leave a lasting legacy of impact, innovation, and humanity. It is this kind of leadership that is not only about the destination, but also about the transformation undertaken — both personally and collectively — along the way.

The Importance of Passion and Grit for an Inspiring Leader

Imagine yourself as a racing driver on a track full of obstacles. At every turn, you face challenges and adversity. What keeps you behind the wheel, propelling you to keep going even when the race gets tough?

The answer is passion and grit burning inside you, like the engine of a sports car. When you're an inspirational leader, these elements are your fuel. Not only do they keep you on track, but they also inspire those who follow you to stay in the race, no matter how steep the climb.

In her book, Angela Duckworth teaches us that passion and perseverance are the key factors for success. This passion is not just a passing interest, but rather the burning flame that propels you to overcome challenges. And just like a racing driver who is passionate about his sport, an inspirational leader is passionate about his mission.

The grip is what keeps you moving forward when the road gets slippery, like the tires of a sports car that grip firmly on the asphalt. An inspirational leader doesn't give up easily; He perseveres when others would give up, as he is committed to his vision and driven by his passion.

Think about how a racing driver, with passion and drive, stays on the track, accelerating no matter how difficult the race gets. Similarly, an inspirational leader maintains their unwavering commitment and determination, showing teams that success is possible as long as the flame of passion and grit is maintained.

In a transformative leadership journey, passion and drive emerge not only as drivers of success, but as the foundations of truly inspiring leadership. Angela Duckworth, in her exploration of grit, reveals that the synergistic combination of persistent passion and dogged perseverance is decisive for achieving long-term success. This passion, far from being a mere passing fascination, burns intensely within the leader, pushing him to face and overcome the challenges inherent to leadership.

Simultaneously, the concepts presented by Simon Sinek and Ryan Holiday in the previous chapters weave a complementary narrative, underlining the importance of a passion that transcends the self, a passion rooted in a broader purpose. Holiday warns us of the dangers of a directionless passion, which, devoid of purpose, can veer into impulsiveness and self-indulgence. On the contrary, a passion anchored in a clear and meaningful purpose—Sinek's "Why"—is able to guide the leader and his team through the turbulent seas of change and uncertainty.

This "Why," which echoes Bill George's teachings on authenticity and Brené Brown's reflections on vulnerability and courage, serves as the north for the inspirational leader. It shapes a leadership that not only aspires to tangible success but also seeks to make a meaningful difference in the world around them by inspiring a culture of authenticity, innovation, and resilience.

Therefore, as we reflect on the importance of passion and grit, it is crucial to recognize that these qualities, when aligned with a deep and authentic purpose, not only propel the leader forward but also ignite the spirit of passion and perseverance in their team. This creates a powerful synergy, in which the leader's vision becomes a shared mission, turning challenges into opportunities for growth, innovation, and collective success.

In this context, the inspirational leader acts as the conductor of an orchestra, in which each member is vital to the final harmony. The leader's passion, grit, and purpose aren't just the fuel that keeps him in the race; They are the music that inspires and moves everyone around them to reach unimaginable heights together.

In short, true Inspirational Leadership is one that recognizes passion and drive not as ends in themselves, but as means to achieve a greater purpose—a purpose that should resonate with each team member, uniting them in a common mission. It is this union of passion, purpose and people that defines the legacy of a truly inspiring leader, transforming the journey into a symphony of shared successes and leaving an indelible mark on the fabric of the world.

Schematized Summary of the Chapter

1. Core Concept: Passion and Perseverance in Leadership

- **What it is:** Passion is an intense and lasting feeling that drives a leader's actions, while perseverance is the ability to stay focused even in the face of obstacles.
- **Why it matters:** The combination of passion and perseverance, or "grit" as defined by Angela Duckworth, is critical to the long-term success of a leader and their team.
- **Practical example:** Nelson Mandela, with his passion for justice and perseverance, inspired a nation to overcome racial segregation.

2. Key elements

- **Passion:** An intense and lasting feeling that drives the leader and his team.

- **Perseverance:** The ability to maintain focus and effort even in the face of challenges.
- **Purpose:** A clear and meaningful goal that guides passion and perseverance.
- **Authenticity:** The genuineness of passion, which manifests itself in coherent actions and attitudes.
- **Resilience:** The ability to bounce back from failures and keep moving forward.

3. Implications and Applications

- **Leadership:** Passionate and persevering leaders inspire their teams and create more engaged and resilient organizational cultures.
- **Personal development:** Passion and perseverance are skills that can be developed and improved in anyone.
- **Organizational success:** Companies led by passionate and determined people tend to be more innovative and resilient.
- **Social impact:** Passionate leaders can inspire positive change in society.

4. Conclusion

Passion and perseverance are crucial elements for inspirational leadership. By combining these elements with a clear purpose and authenticity, leaders can create a work environment where innovation flourishes, challenges are overcome, and goals are achieved. Passion is the fuel that drives the journey, while perseverance ensures that the destination is reached. Inspiring leaders not only achieve success, but they also leave a lasting legacy, inspiring others to follow in their footsteps.

Keywords: passion, perseverance, authenticity, leadership, purpose, inspiration, resilience, success, organizational culture.

Call to Action: Develop your passion and perseverance to become a more inspiring leader and transform your organization. Explore your purpose and inspire your team to achieve great things.

To reflect

- How do you keep your passion for purpose alive and consistent over time, especially in the face of challenges and adversity? This question encourages the leader to reflect on how to sustain the energy and enthusiasm needed to lead effectively.

- How do you demonstrate grit in your leadership, and how does that influence your team's motivation and resilience? Understand how the combination of passion and perseverance can inspire your team to overcome obstacles and pursue ambitious goals.

- How do you differentiate genuine passion and fleeting excitement in your leadership initiatives? This question encourages the leader to think about the depth and durability of their passion, ensuring that it is guided by a meaningful purpose.

- How is your passion aligned with a higher purpose? How do you communicate this purpose to your team? Thinking about this leads us to reflect on how to connect personal passion with organizational mission to engage and inspire the team.

- How do you balance your passion with pragmatism and realism in daily decisions, to ensure sustainable long-term results? Seek to ensure that passion is guided by a sense of purpose and realism, avoiding impulsiveness and ensuring effective and lasting leadership.

Learn more

DUCKWORTH, Angela. *Grit: The power of passion and perseverance.* Intrínseca, 2017.

HOLIDAY, Ryan. *Ego is the Enemy: The Fight to Master Our Greatest Opponent.* [S.l.]: Portfolio, 2016.

4

INTEGRITY

> *A man of integrity walks safely, but he who follows crooked paths will be discovered.*
> *- Proverbs 10:9 (NIV)*

In a complex and ever-evolving business world, where the rules of the game seem to be always changing, there is one pillar that remains unshaken: integrity. For inspirational leaders, integrity is not just a desirable trait; It is an absolute and non-negotiable obligation. More than simply a moral value, integrity is the backbone of trust, which, in turn, is the foundation of any healthy and productive relationship.

The discussion of the fundamental importance of integrity in building and maintaining trust within organizations deepens significantly by exploring Stephen M.R. Covey's insights in "The Speed of Trust." Covey points out that trust is much more than a desirable quality in interpersonal relationships; It is a critical element that directly influences operational effectiveness and organizational agility. The basis of this trust, as Covey articulates, is integrity—a principle that transcends simple honesty and encompasses a convergence of words and actions, promises and achievements.

Integrity, in this context, is seen not only as a moral foundation, but as a strategic asset that can propel an organization to excellence. Leaders who demonstrate integrity not only in their decisions, but also in their daily interactions, establish a standard of behavior that fosters a work environment based on trust. This, in turn, facilitates collaboration, innovation, and a team's ability to tackle challenges with agility and confidence.

Building this culture of trust starts with leaders who understand and live by their core values, ensuring that their actions are always aligned with those values. When leaders act with integrity, they not only inspire their followers to do the same, but they also create a strong foundation on which trust can be built and maintained. This is especially critical in times of crisis, when trust and integrity are put to the test. Leaders who maintain their integrity in these moments demonstrate an unwavering commitment to their principles, reinforcing trust in their leadership.

In addition, Covey argues that trust derived from integrity has a tangible impact on organizational performance. Teams that trust their leaders and colleagues tend to communicate more effectively, collaborate more freely, and innovate more courageously. This is because trust reduces the barriers of fear and uncertainty, freeing people to focus on performing their tasks and finding creative solutions to problems. In other words, trust accelerates operations and decision-making, while a lack of it can slow or even paralyze an organization's progression.

Therefore, embracing integrity as a core value in leadership is not just a matter of ethics, but a vital strategy for cultivating trust, driving performance, and inspiring organizational excellence. Leaders who practice and promote integrity demonstrate a deep understanding of their role not just as managers of resources or strategies, but as guardians of organizational culture and character. Through integrity, they pave the way for truly inspiring leadership, which empowers individuals and teams to reach their full potential in an environment of mutual respect, trust, and genuine cooperation.

A leader may possess exceptional communication skills, impeccable strategy, and innovative vision, but if they lack integrity, they are likely to fail to inspire and earn the trust of their team. Why? Because integrity is about being consistent in word and deed. It means doing what is right, even when no one is watching, and honoring commitments, even when it is difficult or inconvenient.

Many leaders underestimate the power of integrity, believing that small flaws or deviations are acceptable in the name of the "greater good" or "efficiency." However, these small compromises can quickly erode trust and sabotage the moral fabric of the organization. In contrast, leaders who operate with non-negotiable integrity set a high standard, creating an organizational culture in which honesty, transparency, and accountability are valued and practiced from the top down.

The relationship between ethics and effective leadership is inseparable. Ethical leaders recognize that integrity is not something to be relaxed or negotiated. For them, integrity is not a matter of expediency, but a deep commitment to unwavering principles and values. This ethical approach not only solidifies their position as trusted leaders but also sets a standard for everyone within the organization.

Thus, integrity is a powerful tool for attracting and retaining talent. In an era where employees are increasingly looking for meaning and purpose in their work, many are drawn to organizations that demonstrate integrity and ethics in their operations. By cultivating a culture of integrity, leaders not only improve their organization's reputation but also create an environment where employees feel proud of their work and committed to the company's mission.

Non-negotiable integrity is more than a mantra or slogan; it is the beating heart of effective leadership. Leaders who cultivate and demonstrate integrity earn the respect and loyalty of their team, establish a healthy organizational culture, and above all, accelerate their organization's long-term success. In a world filled with uncertainty and challenges, integrity emerges as the compass that guides and defines true inspirational leaders.

Integrity, as already discussed, is not just a tangential aspect of leadership, but actually occupies a central place in the repertoire of any leader who wants to truly inspire and motivate their team. For inspiring leaders, every decision, interaction, and initiative is an opportunity to reinforce the importance and value of integrity. By doing so, they not only establish a strong foundation of trust but also cultivate a place in which authenticity and true leadership can flourish.

Now, as we look back and reflect on the previous chapters, we see how each element of Inspirational Leadership is interconnected. In the first chapter, we discussed the importance of a purposeful vision. Leaders who have a clear vision also need integrity to uphold that vision and align their actions with it. Integrity serves as the glue that keeps the vision intact, ensuring that daily actions and decisions made are always aligned with the greater purpose.

In the second chapter, we emphasize the energy that passion brings to leadership. But... What would passion be without integrity? Passion without integrity can easily turn into fanaticism or blind pursuit of goals without considering the means used. Integrity ensures that the leader's passion is channeled in a productive and ethical manner, creating a positive and encouraging work environment.

Inspirational leaders recognize that to truly inspire others, they must be living examples of their values and principles. Integrity is what gives substance to your passion and purpose, ensuring that these are not just empty words, but realities lived and breathed every day.

Additionally, inspirational leaders know that integrity is not something that can be "turned off" or "turned on" depending on the situation. It is a daily choice, reaffirmed with each challenge, with each obstacle. By maintaining non-negotiable integrity, these leaders send a clear message to their team: that they can be trusted, that their words and actions are aligned, and that even in the most difficult situations, they will stay true to their values and principles.

Non-negotiable integrity is not just a component of Inspirational Leadership; it is your soul. And as we have seen in previous chapters, every element of leadership, whether vision, passion, or any other trait, is intensified and elevated when grounded in solid, unwavering integrity. Inspirational leaders understand this power and use it to create resilient organizations, loyal teams, and an enduring legacy of positive impact.

The Essence of Authentic Leadership

The leadership journey is fraught with challenges and crossroads, where the decisions made not only shape the course of the business but also define the character of the leader. In "The

Courage to Be Imperfect", Brené Brown sheds light on authenticity as a fundamental pillar in building resilient and effective leadership. That authenticity, she suggests, is not just about being true to oneself, but also about being true to those we lead.

Being authentic is a journey of self-knowledge and self-understanding. It requires a deep dive into our values, beliefs, and principles that shape our actions and decisions. This inner exploration allows a leader to align with a deeper purpose and follow a path that truly resonates with who they are.

However, authenticity is more than just introspection. It is put to the test when we are faced with situations in which our values are challenged. It could be a profitable business proposal that conflicts with our ethical principles, or an unpopular decision that aligns with the company's long-term vision but may not be well received in the short term. In such moments, the true essence of authentic leadership is revealed. Brown emphasizes that by choosing authenticity, we may face resistance and criticism, but it is precisely this courage to stay true to who we are that differentiates truly inspiring leaders.

Authenticity also shapes the way we connect with others. Authentic leadership is not only about being transparent in our actions, but also about creating a place in which others feel safe to be themselves. Brené Brown argues that by being vulnerable and showing our true face, we create bridges of trust and understanding. In a work environment, this translates into more engaged, creative, and loyal teams.

Throughout the book, Brown shares stories and research that underscore the importance of authenticity. She mentions leaders who, by embracing their imperfections and vulnerabilities, have been able to inspire and mobilize people around a common vision. These leaders, even in the face of adversity, never compromised their core values. They understood that in the grand scheme of things, being true to oneself and others is invaluable.

For inspirational leaders, authenticity isn't just an option, it's a responsibility. In an ever-changing world, where distrust in institutions is at an all-time high and transparency is required, being authentic is the only way to build and maintain trust. Leaders who understand and incorporate this into their leadership not only build stronger organizations but also leave a lasting legacy.

Concluding the chapter by reflecting on Brené Brown's words leads us to understand that authenticity is, in fact, the essence of leadership with integrity. By embracing this truth, inspirational leaders not only shape the destiny of their organizations, but also positively influence the lives of the people they touch along their journey. Ultimately, it is this positive and lasting impact that defines true leadership success.

By diving deeply into the concepts of courage and authenticity, we perceive an intricate relationship with the central theme of this chapter: integrity. Authenticity, at its core, is not just about being in harmony with one's values; It is also a statement of integrity. In fact, the three qualities – courage, authenticity and integrity – are inseparable in the domain of Inspirational Leadership.

Courage is the driving force that allows a leader to make decisions based on convictions, even when those decisions are difficult or unpopular. But where does this courage originate? Brené Brown suggests that this strength arises from our authenticity. When a leader is connected and committed to his core values and beliefs, he naturally arms himself with the courage to act in accordance with these principles.

However, authenticity alone is not enough. As the popular adage goes: "Actions speak louder than words." This is where integrity comes in, the act of translating that authenticity into consistent actions. Stephen M.R. Covey, in "The Speed of Trust," describes integrity as doing what you say you're going to do. It is keeping your word and your promises, even when it becomes inconvenient. Authentic leaders, armed with courage, can only fully manifest their leadership when they act with unwavering integrity.

A leader who embodies these three pillars creates an environment in which trust flourishes. Integrity builds trust, and as Covey emphasizes, trust is the catalyst for fast and efficient operations in any organization. On a deeper level, trust also

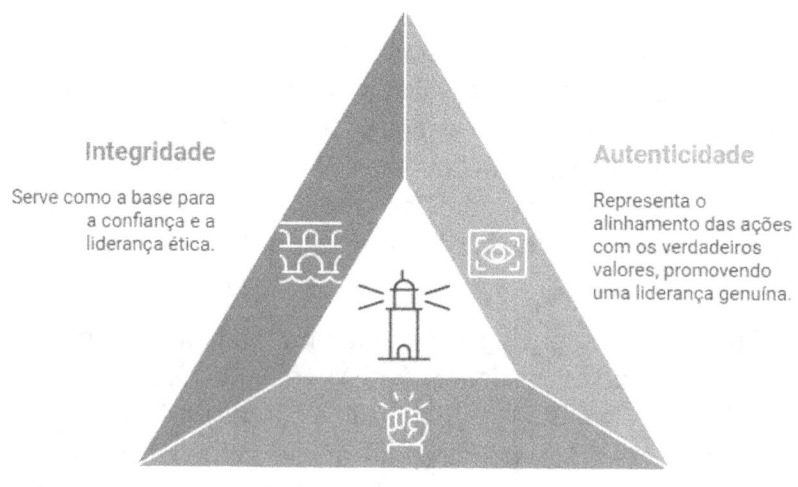

Integridade na Liderança

Integridade
Serve como a base para a confiança e a liderança ética.

Autenticidade
Representa o alinhamento das ações com os verdadeiros valores, promovendo uma liderança genuína.

Coragem
Incorpora a bravura para agir de forma decisiva e inspirar os outros.

becomes the foundation on which genuine and lasting relationships are built, whether with employees, customers, or *stakeholders*.

Having explored the previous themes in this book, we now see how they intertwine. The authentic vision and purpose of an inspirational leader, as emphasized by Simon Sinek and Collins & Porras, finds its ultimate fulfillment when exercised with courage and manifested through leadership of integrity. Authenticity is not a static trait; It requires constant reflection and recalibration to ensure that actions are aligned with the stated values. And at every step of this journey, integrity acts as the beacon, ensuring that the path you choose is always illuminated by the principles that define true leadership.

So, for leaders who want to inspire, the message is clear: authenticity gives rise to courage, and courage, when accompanied by action, is the ultimate proof of integrity. And it is this non-negotiable integrity that stands out as the most admired and influential quality of an inspirational leader. In a world hungry for genuine leadership, those who embrace these principles not only elevate their organizations but also create lasting legacies that transcend time.

Imagine a bridge that crosses a deep chasm, connecting two great peaks. This bridge represents the trust that people place in an inspiring leader. However, this trust is built on a solid foundation called integrity.

Integrity is like the sturdy concrete that supports the bridge of trust. It is the quality of being whole, of being true to oneself and to others. In his book "The Speed of Trust", Stephen M. R. Covey teaches us that trust is the key element for success in any venture, whether in business, family or leadership.

Just as a bridge needs to be built with high-quality materials to stand the test of time, an inspirational leader needs to be built on solid principles of integrity. Trust is born when a leader's words and actions are aligned, when they keep promises, and when they act ethically and responsibly.

Brené Brown, in "The Courage to Be Imperfect," reminds us that integrity involves the courage to be authentic and vulnerable. This means acknowledging our mistakes, learning from them, and constantly seeking to be a better version of ourselves.

Imagine trust as a steel cable that connects the two banks of the bridge. When this steel cable is fragile and corroded by a lack of integrity, the bridge of trust begins to shake and fray. However, when integrity is established, this steel cable is strengthened, making it able to withstand any challenge.

Therefore, integrity is the fundamental pillar that underpins trust in an inspiring leader. Just like a well-built bridge, the trust that comes from integrity allows people to follow the leader with confidence and determination. It is the foundation on which Inspirational Leadership stands, and it is what allows this bridge to successfully connect the dreams and goals of all those who cross it.

Schematized summary of the chapter

1. Core Concept: Integrity in Leadership
- **What it is:** Integrity is the consistency between what you say and what you do, honesty and ethics in all actions.

- **Why it matters:** Integrity is the foundation of trust, which in turn drives team performance and satisfaction.
- **Practical example:** Leaders who act with integrity, such as Nelson Mandela, inspire confidence and loyalty in their followers.

2. Key elements

- **Trust:** Integrity is the foundation of trust, which in turn drives collaboration and innovation.
- **Authenticity:** Integrity requires being authentic, that is, being true to oneself and others.
- **Courage:** Integrity requires courage to make difficult decisions and do what is right, even when it is unpopular.
- **Values:** Integrity is rooted in a set of solid values that guide the leader's actions.

3. Implications and Applications

- **Leadership:** Leaders of integrity inspire confidence, motivation, and loyalty in their teams.
- **Organizational culture:** Integrity shapes a culture of trust, collaboration, and innovation.
- **Decision-making:** Leaders of integrity make decisions that are ethical and aligned with the organization's values.
- **Reputation:** Integrity strengthens the organization's reputation and attracts talent.

4. Conclusion

Integrity is a key pillar of inspirational leadership. By acting with integrity, leaders build trust, inspire their teams, and create a positive work environment. Integrity is not only a desirable quality, but a necessity for those who want to lead effectively and lastingly.

Keywords: integrity, leadership, trust, ethics, values, authenticity, courage, organizational culture.

Call to Action: Leaders, invest in building a reputation for integrity. Be examples of honesty and ethics, and inspire your teams to do the same. Integrity is the foundation on which to build lasting and inspiring leadership.

To reflect

- How do you demonstrate integrity in your daily decisions and interactions with your team? This question encourages the leader to reflect on how their day-to-day actions are aligned with their values and principles.

- How does integrity contribute to building trust within your organization? Focus on the importance of integrity in establishing and maintaining trust between team members and other stakeholders.

- How do you react when your integrity is put to the test, especially in situations of crisis or pressure? This question prompts the leader to consider how he maintains his integrity even in difficult circumstances.

- How does integrity impact organizational culture and attracting talent to your team? Here, we seek to encourage the leader to reflect on how integrity influences the work environment and the reputation of the organization.

- How can you ensure that integrity is a core value not only for you but also for your entire team? Seek to focus on strategies to promote and integrate integrity as a core value throughout the organization.

Learn more

BROWN, Brené. **The Courage to Be Imperfect**. Translated by Joana Angélica d'Avila Melo. Rio de Janeiro: Sextante, 2016.

COVEY, Stephen M.R. **The Speed of Trust: The only one that changes everything**. Translated by Luiz Antonio de Araújo. Rio de Janeiro: Elsevier, 2006.

5

THE ART OF COMMUNICATION IN LEADERSHIP

Communication is the most important leadership skill. Without it, you can't inspire, motivate, or lead.
- John C. Maxwell

"Those who do not communicate, are trumbica." This famous phrase by Abelardo Barbosa, our Chacrinha, could not be more appropriate when it comes to Inspiring Leadership. After all, communication is the foundation on which a leader's success is built, and the absence of it can lead to avoidable stumbles and challenges that could have been overcome more easily.

In this chapter, we will dive deep into the waters of effective communication in leadership. It's not just about avoiding "trumbicar" – facing unnecessary challenges – but also about establishing a solid foundation to strengthen ties and motivate teams. Throughout this journey, we will navigate with the *insights* of renowned authors such as Dale Carnegie, the master behind "How to Win Friends and Influence People," and Nancy Duarte, author of "Resonate," whose ideas illuminate the path of inspiring communication.

Imagine a leader as a skilled pilot in an airplane. Communication is your navigation, your flight instruments, your connection to the control tower. When communication is clear and effective, the plane glides smoothly through the skies, facing turbulence with confidence and precision. However, when communication fails, storm clouds present themselves, and the flight becomes turbulent and uncertain.

In this chapter, we will unravel the secrets of this skillful navigation and teach you how to avoid the storms that arise when communication is poor. Let's explore how communication is key to building strong relationships, motivating teams, and reaching new heights of success.

By the end of this chapter, you'll understand that effective communication is about more than just avoiding problems; It is the wind that sustains the wings of his team, propelling everyone towards the most promising horizons. Join us on this journey through the art of communication in leadership, in which we will learn to avoid "trumbicar" and take higher flights towards inspiring success.

Communication as a Leadership Tool: The Mastery of Inspiration

Imagine a leader as a conductor in front of an orchestra made up of talented musicians. The scene is more than a simple analogy; is a powerful metaphor that illustrates the importance of communication in Inspirational Leadership.

In this context, the leader is the conductor. His baton, much more than a stick, is a tool that expresses his vision, directing the harmony of the group. Just as a conductor seeks to create an engaging and exciting symphony, an inspirational leader seeks to lead his team towards extraordinary goals.

However, the conductor's baton is inert without his ability to communicate. Similarly, a leader needs to communicate clearly and effectively to bring out the best in each member of their team and create a harmonious symphony in their operations.

Dale Carnegie, author of the classic "How to Win Friends and Influence People," offers a valuable lesson here. He underscores the fundamental importance of listening carefully as a starting point for effective communication. Imagine a conductor who does not listen to the musicians of the orchestra. Dissonance would be inevitable, and the desired harmony would turn into chaos.

Listening carefully doesn't just mean listening to the words, but also understanding the emotions, concerns, and perspectives of others. It's an act of empathy that builds the foundation for stronger relationships. Just like a conductor who understands the nuances of his musicians' skills and instruments, a leader who listens comprehensively is better equipped to lead effectively.

Communication is the backbone of Inspirational Leadership. In an ever-changing and evolving world, the ability to connect, influence, and inspire has become an imperative for leaders. However, how exactly does a leader communicate effectively? How does he build bridges, create deep connections, and motivate his team? To answer these questions, we turn to the teachings of two luminaries in the field of communication: Dale Carnegie and Nancy Duarte.

Dale Carnegie, in his timeless work "How to Win Friends and Influence People," offers a map for building meaningful human relationships. He highlights the importance of simple gestures, such as smiling, listening attentively, and recognizing people by their names. However, the core of Carnegie's message lies in his emphasis on empathy, understanding, and genuine understanding. Instead of criticizing, he teaches us to understand. Instead of imposing, he directs us to persuade. It shows us that by valuing and understanding the perspectives of others, we not only build stronger bonds but also broaden our ability to influence and lead.

On the other hand, Nancy Duarte, in "Resonate", takes us on an exploratory journey about the art of presentation and narrative. Duarte believes that the essence of any effective communication is to tell a story that resonates. She emphasizes the need to take the audience on a journey from what "is" to what "can be", creating a contrast that generates tension and engagement. More than simple words, Duarte shows how the integration of *design* and *storytelling* can amplify a message, making it unforgettable.

Diving into the intersection of these two masterful works, we realize that effective communication is actually a combination of interpersonal skills and storytelling skills. Inspirational leaders are those who, as Carnegie suggests, are able to create authentic and deep connections, showing empathy and genuine interest. They are also the ones who, following Duarte's advice, know how to shape and deliver a powerful narrative that inspires action and change.

In a business environment, where teams face constant challenges and motivation can fluctuate, the ability to communicate with clarity and passion becomes vital. Leaders who master these communication techniques and strategies not only strengthen bonds with their team, but also create an atmosphere where the vision is clearly articulated, goals are shared, and everyone feels valued and understood.

As we move into the complexity of the modern world, where information moves at breakneck speeds and interactions become increasingly digital, a question arises with renewed urgency: How can leaders ensure that their messages are not only heard, but also feel a lasting impact?

The answer to this question is multifaceted, but one thing is clear: communication, at its core, is more about listening than talking. Carnegie often emphasized the inestimable value of listening attentively. By truly listening, we not only better understand the other's perspective, but we also sow the seeds of trust and mutual respect. In a corporate environment, this means that leaders must be attentive to their team's concerns, ideas, and feedback. This not only provides valuable *insights* but also reinforces the sense of belonging and value in the team.

Duarte, on the other hand, places a significant focus on the construction of narratives. In the context of leadership, this can be translated into a leader's ability to weave a cohesive and inspiring vision for the future. Stories have the power to unite people under a common goal, providing them with a sense of purpose and direction. And as Duarte points out, it is not only the content of the story that matters, but also how it is told. A well-structured narrative, complemented by effective design and visualization, can elevate a simple message to inspiring heights.

However, while both authors offer valuable strategies, the real power of effective communication lies in the combination of active listening and powerful narration. When leaders adopt a posture of empathy and openness, while articulating their vision with passion and clarity, they create an environment where communication flourishes in all directions.

However, it is important to remember that communication is not a one-time event or a box to be checked. It is an ongoing process that requires practice, reflection, and above all, authenticity. Leaders who are authentic in their communications, who aren't afraid to show vulnerability or admit mistakes, are the ones who truly resonate with their audience.

Ultimately, Inspirational Leadership is a delicate dance between speaking and listening, between guiding and being guided. And while techniques and strategies evolve over time, the fundamental principles remain unchanged: the need for authenticity, empathy, and clarity. In a world where everyone has a voice, the leaders who stand out are those who know when to speak, when to listen, and most importantly, how to do both in a way that resonates deeply with others.

How to improve communication to become an inspirational leader

The art of communication, especially for an inspirational leader, is a skill that requires continuous refinement and dedication. The examples of great communicators show us that communication goes beyond merely transmitting information – it's about creating meaningful connections. For aspiring or current leaders, here is a list of practical actions that can enhance your communication skills:

1) **Listening and Empathy Skills**
    - **Active** Listening: Before speaking, listen. Be fully present in conversations, avoiding distractions and showing genuine interest in what others have to say.
    - **Practice Empathy**: Put yourself in the other person's shoes. Try to understand the emotions, concerns, and perspectives of those around you.
    - **Practice Reflective Listening**: Repeat or rephrase what you heard to confirm understanding and demonstrate that you are really listening.
    - **Avoid Multitasking**: When you're in a conversation or meeting, avoid constantly checking your phone or computer. Give your full attention to communication.

2) **Clarity and Effectiveness in Communication**
    - **Be Clear and Concise**: Avoid jargon or complex language. Convey your message clearly and directly.
    - **Ask for Feedback**: After communicating an idea or direction, ask for feedback to understand if your message was clearly understood.
    - **Use Appropriate Body Language**: Nonverbal communication, such as eye contact, posture, and gestures, plays a crucial role in how the message is perceived.
    - **Be Authentic**: People connect with sincerity. Speak authentically and show your true personality.

3) **Techniques and Continuous Improvement**

- **Study Great Speakers**: Attend speeches and lectures by great communicators. Analyze their techniques, styles, and the way they engage the audience.

- **Participate in Courses and Workshops**: Invest in courses in public speaking, *storytelling* or effective communication. Practice makes perfect.

- **Improve Presentation Skills**: Whether it's through using eye-catching visuals, mastering the art of pausing, or varying your tone of voice, constantly hone your ability to present.

- **Use Stories**: People connect with stories. Use anecdotes and narratives to illustrate points and make your communication more memorable.

4) **Relationship and Work Environment**

- **Foster Safe Environments**: Create spaces where team members feel comfortable sharing their ideas and concerns.

- **Receive Criticism with Grace**: View negative feedback as an opportunity for growth. Thank him and use it to improve.

- **Focus on the Positive**: Start meetings or discussions highlighting the positives or successes, before diving into areas of improvement or concerns.

Regularly implementing and practicing these actions can not only improve a leader's communication skills but also reinforce their ability to lead in an inspiring way. After all, at the heart of Inspirational Leadership is the ability to connect, motivate, and most of all, communicate effectively and compassionately.

Orchestrating Harmony: The Delicate Dance of Inspirational Communication

The Art of Communication in Leadership

Communication is the essence of leadership. As we've seen in previous chapters, understanding the reason for our purpose, the passion that drives our work, and the integrity that underlies our actions all converge on how effectively we communicate these core elements to those we lead. The inspirational leader is not just a speaker; He is a listener, a storyteller and, above all, a builder of bridges between ideas, people and possibilities.

Let's imagine for a moment that the journey of leadership is similar to a dance. In the first chapters, we learn the fundamental steps and the music that moves our spirit. Now, in this chapter, we focus on how we move around the ballroom, ensuring that our dance is seen, felt, and most of all, experienced by all who watch us. Communication is the way we translate the melody of our purpose and the passion of our movement to those around us.

Maybe you remember a time in your life, maybe in your childhood, when you played with a cordless phone. A message would start at one end of the circle, and when it reached the other side, it would often turn into something else entirely. This simple yet revealing game highlights the fragility of communication and how easily messages can be distorted or misunderstood. As leaders, our task is to ensure that the message not only reaches the other side of the circle, but that it gets there with the same clarity and passion with which it began.

To conclude that communication is fundamental to leadership is actually to recognize that leadership is about relationship. And, like any worthwhile relationship, it requires effort, understanding, and, above all, authenticity. So, as we move on to the next chapters, let's remember that whether it's inspiring action, building trust, or creating vision, it all starts with a simple conversation.

Because, at the end of the day, even in the vast and complicated ballroom of life, an inspirational leader knows that the most beautiful dance is the one that is danced with an open heart, inviting everyone to join in and move to the rhythm of the same inspiring melody.

Schematized summary of the chapter

1. Main Concept: Communication as a Leadership Tool

- **What it is:** Effective communication is the ability to convey messages in a clear, concise, and inspiring way, building relationships and motivating teams.

- **Why it matters:** Communication is the bedrock of leadership, allowing leaders to influence, inspire, and unite their teams around a common goal.

- **Practical example:** A conductor conducting an orchestra, using his baton to communicate the musical vision and harmonize the instruments.

2. Key elements

- **Active listening:** Showing genuine interest in what others have to say.

- **Empathy:** Putting yourself in the other person's shoes and understanding their perspectives.

- **Clarity and conciseness:** Convey messages clearly and directly, avoiding jargon.

- **Storytelling:** Using stories to connect with people and inspire.
- **Authenticity:** Being true to yourself and others.
- **Feedback:** Constructively solicit and provide feedback.

3. Implications and Applications

- **Leadership:** Effective communication allows leaders to inspire, motivate, and unite their teams.
- **Interpersonal relationships:** Constructive communication strengthens relationships and creates a positive work environment.
- **Conflict resolution:** Clear communication facilitates conflict resolution and decision-making.
- **Innovation:** Open communication encourages the exchange of ideas and innovation.

4. Conclusion

Effective communication is the key to inspiring leadership. By mastering the skills of active listening, empathy, clarity, and storytelling, leaders can build stronger relationships, motivate their teams, and achieve exceptional results. Communication is not just a tool, but a fundamental element of leadership that allows leaders to connect with people on a deep level and inspire them to achieve great things.

Keywords: communication, leadership, inspiration, active listening, empathy, narrative, authenticity, relationship.

Call to Action: Leaders, invest in improving your communication skills. By listening carefully, communicating clearly, and building authentic relationships, you'll be able to inspire your teams and achieve extraordinary results.

To reflect

- How can the comparison between a leader and a conductor help to understand the importance of effective communication in leadership? Explain how communication drives a team's "symphony" to achieve common goals.

- How does the practice of active listening, as advocated by Dale Carnegie, contribute to strengthening inspirational leadership? Discuss how listening carefully can influence building strong relationships and increase trust within the team.

- How can the use of narratives and storytelling, as suggested by Nancy Duarte, amplify the effectiveness of communication? Give examples of how leaders can use stories to engage and motivate their team.

- What are the essential practices to improve a leader's communication, and how can they be implemented in a work environment? Identify and explain at least three practices discussed in the chapter that can be applied in a leader's day-to-day life.

- Why is communication described as a "delicate dance" in leadership, and how can leaders ensure that their messages are received with clarity and impact? Reflect on the strategies a leader can use to avoid distortions in communication and ensure that their vision is clearly understood by all team members.

Learn more

CARNEGIE, Dale. *How to Win Friends and Influence People*. São Paulo: Companhia Editora Nacional, 1936.

DUARTE, Nancy. *Resonate: Visual Presentations That Transform Audiences*. San Francisco: Wiley, 2010.

6

EMPATHY AND ENGAGEMENT

> *Leadership is about empathy. It's about having the ability to relate and connect with people to inspire and empower them.*
> *- Oprah Winfrey*

At the heart of Inspirational Leadership, we find two intrinsic components that shape a leader's effectiveness and impact: empathy and engagement. By embracing and understanding the interconnectedness of these elements, leaders can unleash incredible potential not only within themselves, but also in their teams.

Brené Brown, in her revealing work "The Courage to Be Imperfect", leads us to a profound discovery about the value of vulnerability and human connection. Behind their approach lies a fundamental truth that all inspirational leaders must recognize: vulnerability is not a weakness, but a strength.

It is the gateway to empathy, and empathy is the foundation of true leadership.

In today's business world, where perfection is often the desired standard, vulnerability can seem counterintuitive. However, Brown argues that it is precisely by recognizing and accepting our imperfections that we can authentically connect with others. And it is in this authenticity that empathy flourishes. Empathy is the ability to feel with someone, not just for someone. And for a leader, it's this ability to "feel with" that creates fertile ground for deep and meaningful engagement.

Imagine a team where every member feels they are seen, heard, and valued. In which every challenge, failure or success is shared and experienced collectively. That's the power of empathy in action. By creating an environment where vulnerability is embraced and empathy is cultivated, leaders not only strengthen their team's bonds, but also foster deep and lasting engagement.

But what does it really mean to be engaged? In the context of Brown's approach, engagement is the visible manifestation of genuine connection. It is the natural result of feeling that we belong to something bigger than ourselves and that our contribution is valuable and meaningful. And, crucially, it's driven by empathy. When a leader empathizes, it sends a clear message: "I understand. I care. We're in this together."

Engagement is not something that can be forced or imposed. It's something that comes naturally when empathy is the norm and vulnerability is seen as courage. And for leaders seeking to inspire, this is an invaluable lesson.

When reflecting on the leadership journey, it is vital to recognize that more than strategies, tactics, or technical skills, it is the ability to connect with others on a human and emotional level that defines a truly inspiring leader. Because, as Brown so eloquently reminds us, at the end of the day, we are all imperfect, but it is in our shared imperfection that we find our collective strength and purpose. And it is through empathy and engagement that we lead, not only with the mind, but more importantly, with the heart.

As we dive deeper into the essence of what it means to lead, it becomes evident that at the core of Inspirational Leadership is not the ability to give orders or direct, but rather the ability to understand, connect, and most of all, care. Leaders who walk this path are not only respected; they are loved, and the difference is palpable.

Brené Brown also teaches us that empathy is not a passive act, but an active choice. Choosing to be empathetic in a world that often values emotional distance and objectivity requires courage. But that courage has priceless rewards. Teams led with empathy not only work more effectively, but they also feel more invested in their mission and each of their members. That emotional investment is what leads to innovation, resilience, and ultimately, lasting success.

However, it is vital to understand that empathy and engagement are not finish lines, but rather continuous journeys. An inspirational leader is constantly looking for ways to connect more deeply, to understand better, and to create spaces in which each individual feels valued and understood. Leadership is not a monologue, but a constant dialogue, an exchange of ideas, feelings, and aspirations.

In addition, by creating a space in which vulnerability is welcomed, inspiring leaders also cultivate an environment of continuous learning and growth. After all, it is only when we allow ourselves to be vulnerable, recognizing our mistakes and failures, that we truly learn and evolve. This environment of authenticity and growth becomes a magnet for talent and an inexhaustible source of innovation.

As we look back at the previous chapters, we see an intricate tapestry of values, principles, and practices that form the foundation of Inspirational Leadership. And as we move forward, it's crucial to remember that at the heart of this tapestry is empathy and engagement. They are the ones who give life and color to each thread, making leadership not just a function, but an art.

And so we conclude this chapter with a simple but powerful reflection: imagine a world in which every leader chooses, every day, to lead from the heart, in which empathy is not the exception but the rule. A world where each person feels seen, heard and valued. This is the world an inspirational leader seeks to create, one step, one conversation, and one connection at a time. And while that journey is never easy, the rewards, as shown by the stars in the darkest sky, are endless and absolutely dazzling.

Empathy and engagement are not only popular themes in contemporary leadership literature; They have been the foundation upon which great leaders and thinkers throughout history have built their legacies.

Nelson Mandela, anti-apartheid leader and former president of South Africa, once remarked, "Leading by example is not the primary way to influence others. It's the only way." His life exemplified the intimate connection between leadership, empathy, and engagement. Mandela showed the world that by putting yourself in the shoes of others, by feeling their pain and understanding their hopes, it is possible to lead in ways that unify and inspire nations.

Mahatma Gandhi, another leader whose legacy is synonymous with compassion and empathy, taught, "You must be the change you want to see in the world." This quote underscores the importance of active engagement. It is not enough to desire change or talk about it; It is necessary to live them, feel them intensely and guide others by example.

Stephen R. Covey, author of "The 7 Habits of Highly Effective People," highlighted the importance of empathy in his words: "Seek first to understand, then to be understood." This is a call to active listening, to really connect with others on a deep level before pursuing our own goals.

And Maya Angelou, whose words continue to inspire generations, reminds us of the enduring importance of empathy and engagement when she says, "People will forget what you said, people will forget what you did, but people will never forget how you made them feel." Inspirational leadership is ultimately about creating lasting feelings of belonging, value, and understanding.

Howard Schultz, former CEO of Starbucks, a company known for its focus on human connection, noted, "A company's most precious value is its self-image, its self-esteem, and its philosophy of existence. You get that only if you build a company based on people, empathy, respect and mutual understanding."

These words, from such varied leaders and thinkers, offer us a window into the soul of Inspirational Leadership. They underscore a truth that remains constant through time and culture: at the center of every great leader, there is a heart that understands, feels, and connects. And it's that genuine connection, that deep engagement, and that unwavering empathy that turns followers into advocates, visions into realities, and dreams into lasting legacies. In a world filled with noise and distractions, the ability to connect heart-to-heart is what sets truly inspiring leaders apart.

The Journey to Connection: Essential Practices for Empathetic and Engaged Leaders

To lead with authentic empathy and foster genuine team engagement, an inspirational leader must internalize and practice tangible actions. Here is a list of actions that can transform leadership style and create a more connected and inspiring work environment:

1. **Practice Active Listening:** Focus completely on the speaker, understanding, responding, and then remembering the conversation. This means avoiding interruptions and really listening to what's being said.

2. **Show Genuine Interest:** Ask open-ended questions that encourage team members to share more about themselves and their perspectives.

3. **Establish Personal Connections:** Take the time to get to know your team outside of a strictly professional context. It could be a casual lunch or team-building events.

4. **Be open about your feelings:** When appropriate, share your emotions and concerns, showing that you are also human and vulnerable.

5. **Encourage Feedback:** Create a safe environment for staff to express opinions, concerns, and ideas without fear of reprimand.

6. **Recognize and Value Differences:** Understand that each person brings a unique perspective to the table. Instead of suppressing these differences, embrace them.

7. **Practice Daily Reflection:** Take time each day to reflect on your interactions, identify areas for improvement, and recognize times when you have shown true empathy.

8. **Promote Continuous Learning:** Encourage staff (and yourself) to attend workshops and training on emotional intelligence, effective communication, and interpersonal skills.

9. **Show Gratitude:** A simple "thank you" can do wonders for an individual's morale and sense of belonging.

10. **Apologize When Necessary:** Acknowledge your mistakes and apologize sincerely. This shows humility and authenticity.

11. **Set Clear Boundaries:** While empathy is essential, it is also important to set clear boundaries to ensure mutual respect and efficiency.

12. **Celebrate Team Victories:** Recognize and celebrate achievements, big and small. This not only reinforces the sense of belonging but also demonstrates appreciation.

13. **Promote Mental Health:** Encourage breaks, provide resources, and be an advocate for your team's emotional well-being.

14. **Be Present:** In a world dominated by digital devices and multitasking, simply being present during interactions can have a profound impact.

15. **Establish a Clear Purpose:** Ensure that each team member understands the larger purpose behind the work they are doing. This creates a sense of belonging and direction.

By implementing these actions, leaders not only reinforce their empathy and engagement, but also sow the seeds of an organizational culture where everyone feels valued, understood, and inspired to give their best every day. And, as great leaders have taught us throughout history, it is this human connection that is the very essence of Inspirational Leadership.

Build Bridges with Empathy for Inspiring Leadership

Throughout our journey exploring the essence of Inspirational Leadership, we realize that each chapter, each teaching, is like a brick in the construction of a monumental building. We started with the importance of a clear purpose and unwavering passion, moved on to integrity and authenticity, and now we get to the heart of it all: empathy and engagement.

In the world of architecture, a building is only as strong as its foundation. Effective communication, vulnerability, and integrity are key, but it's empathy and engagement that tie it all together, working like the cement that holds the bricks together. It is this combination that gives the building its true strength and durability.

Imagine yourself walking through a forest. Around it, towering trees rise, each different, but all part of a complex and interconnected ecosystem. Just like these trees, each member of a team, with their unique skills, passions, and experiences, contributes to the flourishing of the whole. But it's empathy that allows you to feel the forest, understand its nuances, and ensure that every tree, every individual, flourishes to its fullest potential.

Empathy and engagement, therefore, are not merely desirable traits in a leader; are essential. They are the bridge that connects the leader's vision to the team's passion, turning ideas into actions, dreams into realities.

As we reflect on what we have learned so far, it is clear that true leadership is not an act of dominating but of serving; It's not about standing out, but about elevating others. And in the end, an inspirational leader is one who, through their empathy and engagement, manages to light the way, not only for themselves, but for everyone who has the privilege of walking alongside them.

So, as we prepare for the next chapters of this journey of discovery, let us always remember the words of Maya Angelou: "People will never forget how you made them feel." In a world filled with noise, pressure, and challenges, it may be the ability to make someone feel seen, heard, and valued that makes the most lasting mark. And this, in its purest essence, is the true art of Inspirational Leadership.

Schematized summary of the chapter

1. Main Concept: Empathy and Engagement

- **What it is:** Empathy is the ability to put yourself in the other's shoes and understand their emotions and perspectives. Engagement is the result of the emotional connection between leader and team, leading to greater commitment and motivation.

- **Why it matters:** Empathy and engagement are crucial for building strong relationships, creating a positive work environment, and achieving organizational success.
- **Practical example:** A leader who demonstrates empathy by listening to an employee's concerns and offering support creates an environment of trust and collaboration.

2. Key elements

- **Vulnerability:** The courage to be vulnerable and recognize one's own imperfections.
- **Connection:** The ability to build authentic and meaningful relationships with team members.
- **Trust:** The trust that develops when team members feel understood and valued.
- **Motivation:** Engagement leads to greater motivation and commitment to the team's goals.
- **Innovation:** An empathetic and engaged work environment fosters creativity and innovation.

3. Implications and Applications

- **Leadership:** Empathetic and engaged leaders inspire their teams and achieve better results.
- **Organizational culture:** Empathy and engagement create a positive and collaborative culture.
- **Team development:** Empathy facilitates the development of cohesive and effective teams.
- **Well-being:** An empathetic work environment contributes to employee well-being.

4. Conclusion

Empathy and engagement are fundamental pillars of Inspirational Leadership. By cultivating these qualities, leaders create an environment where people feel valued, motivated, and committed to the organization's success. The ability to connect with others on a deep level and to build authentic relationships is what differentiates an inspirational leader from a mere manager.

Keywords: empathy, engagement, leadership, vulnerability, connection, trust, motivation, organizational culture.

Call to Action: Leaders, invest in developing your empathy and creating a work environment where everyone feels valued and engaged. By doing so, you'll not only build stronger teams, but you'll also achieve more meaningful and lasting results.

To reflect

- How can vulnerability be a strength rather than a weakness in inspirational leadership? With the aim of leading to reflection on the role of vulnerability in building authentic and trusting connections within the team.

- In what ways can empathy impact a team's engagement? Explore how practicing leader empathy can create a more collaborative and motivating environment.

- What is the difference between feeling empathy for someone and feeling empathy for someone? How does this influence team dynamics? Highlight the importance of a deeper and more authentic connection, which goes beyond simply understanding the difficulties of others.

- What daily practices can you adopt to increase your level of empathy and engagement with your team? How to encourage the practical implementation of actions that reinforce the connection and engagement between leader and team.

- How can a leader balance the need to make quick and intuitive decisions with the importance of careful and empathetic reflection? It challenges the leader to think about how to integrate intuition with empathy in decision-making, ensuring that they are fair and well-founded.

Learn more

ANGELOU, Maya. *I Know Why the Bird Sings in the Cage*. São Paulo: Editora Astral Cultural, 2018.

BROWN, Brené. *The Courage to Be Imperfect*. Rio de Janeiro: Sextante, 2012.

COVEY, Stephen R. *The 7 Habits of Highly Effective People*. São Paulo: Editora Best Seller, 1989.

GANDHI, Mahatma. My Life and My Experiences with Truth. São Paulo: Editora Palas Athena, 2007.

MANDELA, Nelson. Long Walk to Freedom: Autobiography of Nelson Mandela. São Paulo: Globo, 1995.

7

DECISION AND DIRECTION

> *The key to a good decision is a balanced assessment of all available information, combined with the courage to follow one's intuition when necessary.*
> *— John C. Maxwell*

On any journey, whether personal or professional, decisions must be made. These decisions set the course of the trajectory and set the pace for results. As inspirational leaders, our ability to make assertive decisions and provide clear direction is critical. After all, it's these decisions that shape the future of our team and the realization of our vision.

Malcolm Gladwell, in his fascinating book "Blink: The Decision at a Blink of an Eye", presents an in-depth study of the decision-making process. It taps into the intriguing gift we all possess – the ability to evaluate and act in a matter of seconds. Gladwell shows us how, often, a mere "blink of an eye" is all it takes to identify the essence of a situation and take the right action.

But what does this have to do with inspirational leadership? Much more than we can initially imagine. Leaders are constantly in a whirlwind of decisions. From seemingly insignificant everyday choices to strategic decisions that can define the fate of an organization. And in the midst of this turmoil, how do we ensure that we are making the right decisions?

Gladwell points in an interesting direction. He suggests that our intuition, that guttural feeling we have about something, is not just a mere guess. It is a rich tapestry of experiences, knowledge, and insight that our brain weaves in milliseconds. And this ability to "think thin," as he puts it, is often as accurate as detailed analysis.

The message is clear: intuition is powerful, it is not infallible.

For inspirational leaders, this dichotomy presents a challenge. How do you balance this incredible ability to make quick decisions with the discernment needed to ensure that the decision is the right one? And more, how to convey this decision clearly and decisively to the team, ensuring that everyone is aligned and moving in the same direction?

The answer lies in understanding that while intuition is a valuable tool, it is only one of many in our leadership arsenal. It is crucial to create an environment where team members are comfortable questioning and challenging decisions, thus ensuring a balance between quick action and careful reflection.

Providing clear direction is not just the act of making a decision and communicating it. It's about creating a sense of purpose and passion that resonates with each team member. And, as Gladwell deftly reminds us through his captivating narratives, it's about trusting, but also questioning, our instincts.

On our journey to becoming inspirational leaders, we must learn to embrace the magic of the "blink of an eye," while also nurturing a culture of open dialogue and healthy questioning. For, as history and research have shown us, when we combine the speed of intuition with the depth of reflection, we are able to create wonders.

As we approach the end of this chapter, reflect on the decisions you have made recently. Which of them were instinctive and which were the result of deep reflection? And more importantly, how can you use the *insights* in this chapter to make better decisions and provide clearer direction in the future?

Always remember: it is in the encounter between intuition and reflection that we discover the true art of deciding and leading. And that's where the inspirational leader truly shines. In a world of endless choices and paths, being the beacon that guides your team with clarity and purpose is what defines true Inspirational Leadership.

Continuing to explore the concepts of decision and direction, it is essential to recognize that decisions made by inspirational leaders are not just for their own benefit or to score points. They are designed to serve a greater purpose, for the good of all under their leadership, and often for the common good.

Every decision made carries the weight of its consequences, both positive and negative. Inspirational leaders understand this and strive to ensure that their decisions, even when made in the blink of an eye, are informed, fair, and aligned with the organization's values and vision.

There is a beauty in the ability to trust one's intuition. But there is also an art to the ability to recognize when that intuition needs to be checked, challenged, and weighed against additional information. And in the midst of all this, transparency in communication plays a crucial role. After all, a decision, no matter how correct or intuitive it may seem, is useless if it is not communicated and understood.

As we look back, we see the topics covered in previous chapters, such as empathy, communication, integrity, and authenticity. These are not just isolated attributes; They are intrinsically linked to the way we decide and direct. Empathy informs our decisions, ensuring that we consider everyone affected by them. Communication ensures that these decisions are understood and accepted. Integrity and authenticity ensure that our decisions are truthful and consistent with our vision and values.

And in all these actions and decisions, the wisdom of great leaders and thinkers who came before us resonates. As Steve Jobs told us,

> *Your work will fill a large part of your life, and the only way to be truly satisfied is to do what you believe to be great work. And the only way to do great work is to love what you do.*

This passion, this love for what we do, serves as a compass, guiding every decision we make.

As inspirational leaders, our ultimate goal is not just to make decisions, but to make decisions that inspire, uplift, and move people toward a greater goal. By doing so, we create more than just successful teams or companies; We create legacies.

So, as we move forward, each inspirational leader must ask themselves, "What kind of legacy do I want to leave?" The answer to this question should serve as a guide, illuminating every decision and direction we take.

And so, like a navigator guided by the stars on a dark night, we must trust our intuition, equipped with the knowledge and wisdom gained along the way, and move forward with courage, passion, and purpose. Because, in the end, it is the journey of leading with decision and clear direction that transforms the ordinary into the extraordinary. And this transformation is the true essence of Inspirational Leadership.

Within the leadership universe, a number of great minds have stood out, each contributing deep *insights* and insights into the attributes crucial to effective leadership. Empathy and engagement have always emerged as core qualities that differentiate good leaders from truly exceptional leaders.

Nelson Mandela, one of the most revered leaders of the twentieth century, often spoke about the importance of empathy and mutual understanding. He noted, "Leadership involves listening and learning." Mandela understood that leading is not just giving orders; it is understanding the needs and feelings of others in order to better serve and guide. His leadership was defined by his ability to connect with those he led, in a deeply human and empathetic way.

Similarly, Stephen R. Covey, in his influential book "The 7 Habits of Highly Effective People," discusses the need to understand before being understood. Covey pointed out, "Most people don't listen with the intention of understanding; they listen with the intention of responding." This is a powerful reflection on the need for authentic empathy and genuine attention when communicating as a leader.

Legendary business leader Richard Branson echoed this same sensibility across his multiple companies, claiming that "I listen. I listen. I listen. And then I ask some question, and then I listen more." Branson recognizes that the foundation for any effective engagement is, first and foremost, a deep understanding.

Such reflections hark back to the observation of poet and civil rights activist/advocate Maya Angelou, who said, "I've learned that people will forget what you said, people will forget what you did, but people will never forget how you made them feel." True empathy creates a lasting impact, establishing fertile ground for engagement and deep connection.

Great leaders past and present understand that the ability to connect with others, to feel what they feel, and to understand their perspectives, is not only a useful skill, but an essential one. Leadership is not just about strategizing or achieving goals. At the heart of leadership lies humanity. And it is empathy and genuine engagement that allow this humanity to shine.

Within the context of engagement, it is always good to remember what Simon Sinek, author and motivational speaker, stresses: "People don't buy what you do, they buy why you do it." To truly engage, it is necessary to communicate not only what and how, but, more crucially, why. Purpose is the foundation of authentic engagement.

Inspiring leaders not only recognize the importance of empathy and engagement, but practice them as the foundation of their leadership. They know that in order to inspire and guide effectively, one must first understand and connect. And it is this deep human connection that becomes the true driving force behind any transformative leadership.

The Compass of Understanding

As we trace our journey through the essence of Inspirational Leadership, we clearly see that leadership is more than just a series of actions or decisions made; It's about connections. Connections with purposes, values, visions and, most imperatively, connections with people. Leadership is not a solitary act; It's a dance. And each step of this dance, as we have seen throughout the previous chapters, requires a meticulous balance between passion and purpose, between integrity and authenticity, and between communication and understanding.

Empathy and engagement, discussed in this chapter, are the link that unites all these elements. They are the fuel that feeds the flame of Inspirational Leadership. After all, a leader without empathy is like a ship without a compass, adrift in a vast ocean. And a leader who does not engage is like a conductor without an orchestra, moving the baton in the void.

We recall the words of great leaders and thinkers, from Mandela to Branson, from Covey to Angelou, and we see a common thread – the unwavering belief in the ability and necessity to connect with others. They taught us that leadership, at its purest essence, is about humanity.

As we reflect on this journey, we are reminded of a simple but powerful metaphor – that of the river. Each river, at its source, is small and insignificant. But as it progresses, it is fed by tributaries, grows in strength and purpose, and finally becomes a powerful force of nature. Just like a river, a leader starts small, but with every experience, with every connection, and with every act of empathy and engagement, he grows, becomes more powerful, and ultimately leaves an indelible mark on the world around him.

And so, as we prepare to embark on the next chapters of our exploration of leadership, we take with us a simple but profound truth: that at the heart of every great leader is a genuine desire to understand and be understood. And, like the river that strives to reach the ocean, it is this never-ending search for connection that drives us, inspires us, and guides us on our journey.

To end with a reflection, in the words of the acclaimed poet Rumi: "The river that flows in you also flows in me." And this, dear readers, is one of the foundations of Inspirational Leadership – recognizing that what flows in us flows in everyone. And it is this understanding that guides, enlightens and inspires us.

Schematized summary of the chapter

1. Main Concept: Decision Making in Leadership

- **What it is:** Decision-making is the process of choosing between different options, defining the course of action of a leader and their team.
- **Why it matters:** The ability to make assertive decisions and provide clear direction is critical to the success of any leader.
- **Practical example:** A CEO deciding on the launch of a new product, evaluating the risks and benefits, and communicating the decision to the team.

2. Key elements

- **Intuition:** The ability to make quick and effective decisions based on prior experience and knowledge.
- **Analytics:** The ability to collect and analyze data to make informed decisions.

- **Communication:** The ability to communicate decisions in a clear and inspiring way to the team.
- **Purpose:** The alignment of decisions with the vision and values of the organization.

3. Implications and Applications

- **Leadership:** Leaders who make effective decisions inspire confidence and motivate their teams.
- **Strategy:** Decision-making is critical to formulating and implementing effective strategies.
- **Organizational culture:** The way decisions are made influences the culture of the organization.
- **Innovation:** The ability to make decisions that are quick and adapted to change is crucial for innovation.

4. Conclusion

Decision-making is an essential skill for any leader. By combining intuition with analysis, clear communication, and alignment with purpose, leaders can make more effective decisions and inspire their teams to achieve extraordinary results.

Keywords: decision, leadership, intuition, analysis, communication, purpose, vision, strategy, organizational culture.

Call to Action: Leaders, develop your ability to make assertive decisions and inspire confidence in your teams. By combining intuition, analysis, and clear communication, you can guide your organizations to a brighter future.

To reflect

- How can you balance intuition and careful reflection when making decisions that affect your team and organization? It encourages the leader to think about how to integrate the quickness of intuition with the depth of reflection to make informed decisions.

- In what ways can communicating clear direction influence team alignment and motivation? Explore the importance of communicating not only the decision, but also the purpose and vision behind it, to engage the team.

- What are the risks of relying solely on intuition for decision-making? How can you mitigate them? Reflect on the limits of intuition and the importance of validating quick decisions with additional information and feedback from the team.

- How can you create an environment where your team feels comfortable questioning and challenging their decisions? Encourage the creation of a culture of open dialogue and feedback, which strengthens the decision-making process and team involvement.

- When should you prioritize speed in decision-making, and when is it necessary to invest more time in reflection? It challenges the leader to identify situations where quick action is essential and others where more careful analysis is needed to ensure effective decisions.

Learn more

BROWN, Brené. **The courage to be imperfect.** São Paulo: Sextante, 2016.

CARNEGIE, Dale. **How to win friends and influence people.** São Paulo: Companhia Editora Nacional, 2012.

COVEY, Stephen R. **The 7 habits of highly effective people.** São Paulo: Best Seller, 2005.

DUARTE, Nancy. **Resonate: visual presentations that transform audiences.** Rio de Janeiro: Alta Books, 2013.

GLADWELL, Malcolm. **Blink: the decision in the blink of an eye.** São Paulo: Editora Objetiva, 2005.

MANDELA, Nelson. **Long walk to freedom.** São Paulo: Editora Globo, 1995.

RUMI, Jalāl al-Dīn. **The essential book of the poet who saw God.** São Paulo: Attar Editorial, 2005.

8

Continued Growth

> *The mind that opens itself to a new idea will never return to its original size.*
> *- Albert Einstein*

In the vast universe of leadership, technical skills and innate ability have their value. However, one key but often underestimated trait comes to the fore when it comes to leadership excellence: mindset. And this is where Carol S. Dweck, in her acclaimed work "Mindset: The New Psychology of Success", unravels the potent magic of the growth mindset, challenging traditional assumptions about success and talent.

Each leader has their own trajectory, full of triumphs, challenges and, sometimes, failures. However, as Dweck astutely points out, it is not the event itself, but our response to it that determines our true potential. Leaders who adopt a rigid mindset may see challenges as insurmountable barriers or failures as reflections of their inaptitudes. On the other hand, leaders with a growth mindset see such obstacles as opportunities, moments to learn, adapt and evolve.

In the business realm, this growth mindset transcends the individual leader and can infuse an organizational culture. Imagine a company where every failure is not a dead end but a springboard for innovation. Imagine a team where each member sees challenges not as threats, but as opportunities to grow. It is this insight that Dweck brings us, and its relevance to inspirational leaders is invaluable.

But how can a leader cultivate this growth mindset in themselves and, by extension, in their team? First, it is essential to understand what skills can be developed. Rather than adopting the belief that intelligence or talent are static qualities, inspirational leaders embrace the idea that with the right effort, strategy, and resources, any skill can be improved. This is a powerful perspective, as it allows leaders and their teams to face challenges with optimism and resilience.

In addition, communication plays a crucial role. The way leaders provide feedback, recognize efforts, and encourage the team can fuel a growth mindset. For example, instead of praising a team member's innate intelligence or talent, a leader may recognize the effort and strategy employed, thereby encouraging a growth approach.

Dweck also highlights the importance of valuing the process, not just the result. In a work environment, this can translate into celebrating the efforts and steps along the way, not just the final triumphs. By doing so, leaders establish a culture where the journey is as valued as the destination, where every challenge is seen as a valuable part of the growth process.

Now, bringing it into the context of Inspirational Leadership, the beauty of the growth mindset lies in its universality. No matter where you are in your leadership journey, whether you're a young leader starting out or a veteran with decades of experience, the growth mindset offers a lens through which you can see the world richer, more complex, and full of possibilities.

And for aspiring leaders, herein lies a potent message: Your journey never truly ends. With a growth mindset, every day brings a new opportunity to learn, grow, and become an even better version of yourself.

Ultimately, as we navigate the turbulent seas of leadership, Dweck's growth mindset emerges like a beacon, lighting the way and reminding us that with the right mindset, horizons are truly limitless. And for an inspirational leader, such a mindset is not just a tool, but the very beating heart of transformative leadership.

As we reflect on the teachings of the previous chapters and look to the future, we are reminded of a simple yet powerful truth: "At the heart of every inspirational leader lies the relentless pursuit of growth—not just growth in numbers or successes, but growth of spirit, mind, and heart." And it is this pursuit that ultimately defines the true essence of Inspirational Leadership.

As we move through the complex web of leadership, Dweck's core message becomes evident: it is not the finish line that defines a leader, but rather the journey and the way they face obstacles along the way. The ability to persist in the face of adversity, to pick yourself up after a fall, and to continue with an unwavering belief in the potential for growth is what separates ordinary leaders from truly inspiring leaders.

Great leaders in history, from Nelson Mandela to Mahatma Gandhi, have demonstrated this growth mentality in their actions. They faced unimaginable adversity, but instead of surrendering or straying from their paths, they used these challenges as stepping stones for learning and innovation. As Mandela once declared, "I never lose. Either I win or I learn." This is the essence of the growth mindset encapsulated in a single powerful sentence.

The true test of leadership does not occur when everything is going well, but rather when the cards are stacked against you. It is in these crucial moments that the growth mindset becomes your greatest ally. Instead of seeing challenges as insurmountable, an inspirational leader sees them as opportunities for growth, learning, and innovation.

To integrate this mindset into a team or organization, it is critical to create an environment in which mistakes are not only tolerated, but celebrated as learning opportunities. A culture where questioning, innovating, and taking calculated risks are encouraged. In which each team member is empowered to reach their full potential, armed with the belief that with the right effort and dedication, growth is always possible.

In retrospect, the previous chapters of this book laid the foundation for effective leadership, addressing topics such as purpose, passion, integrity, communication, empathy, and engagement. However, all of these elements converge on the central idea of this chapter: the growth mindset. Because, at the end of the day, Inspirational Leadership is an ongoing journey of self-discovery, learning, and growth.

Let us remember that true greatness is not defined by the destination, but by the journey. Like a tree that grows continuously, seeking the sun and extending its roots deeper into the earth, an inspirational leader is one who, regardless of adversity, relentlessly strives for growth and excellence. In an ever-changing world, it is this adaptability, this insatiable pursuit of learning and evolution, that defines the true art of Inspirational Leadership. And, as the ancient Chinese proverb reminds us, "The best time to plant a tree was twenty years ago. The second best time is now." So, whatever stage of your leadership journey, it's always the right time to adopt the growth mindset and start cultivating your limitless potential.

Flying with Giants: Great Leaders' Wisdom on Continuous Growth

Throughout history, the most remarkable and transformative leaders have been those who have embraced the idea of continuous growth, understanding that true leadership is not a destination, but rather a journey. They understood that, just as a plant does not stop growing until it reaches its full height, a leader never stops learning, evolving and adapting.

Mahatma Gandhi, the eternal advocate of nonviolence and leader of Indian independence, proclaimed, *"Live as if you were going to die tomorrow. Learn as if you were going to live forever."* This statement not only emphasizes the importance of absorbing knowledge but also the inestimable value of continuous learning.

Nelson Mandela, whose resilience and dedication to justice and equality transformed a nation, once remarked, *"I fear no failure. I'm afraid I'll stop trying."* Mandela understood that growth can only be achieved through continuous effort, regardless of the adversities faced.

Leonardo da Vinci, one of the most well-known and versatile Renaissance geniuses, declared, *"Learning never exhausts the mind."* In an era of insatiable curiosity, Da Vinci embodied the growth mindset, always seeking to understand more, regardless of the area of knowledge.

John C. Maxwell, a renowned author and speaker on leadership, captured the essence of continuous growth when he said, *"If you're growing, you're always out of your comfort zone."* Maxwell reminds us that growing up, by nature, challenges the *status quo* and requires courage to step out of the familiar.

And it's impossible to talk about the growth mindset without mentioning Carol S. Dweck, who has delved into this idea in her work. She states:

> *In a fixed mindset, people believe that their basic qualities, such as intelligence or talent, are fixed traits. In a growth mindset, people understand that their skills and intelligence can be developed with dedication and effort.*

All of these voices, from different eras, cultures, and domains, converge on a single truth: continuous growth is the essence of great leadership. They remind us that leadership is not just about where you are right now, but where you are striving to go. True Inspirational Leadership is a continuous dance of learning, adaptation, and evolution.

As aspiring or established leaders, we can draw inspiration from these words and adopt a posture of curiosity, openness, and determination. History repeatedly shows us that the most impactful leaders are those who, regardless of the achievements achieved, remain humble students in the school of life. And so, as we continue to navigate the challenges and triumphs of leadership, let us always hold in our hearts the idea that growth, in its purest and most powerful form, is truly never-ending.

In the Footsteps of Giants – The Eternal Dance of Growth

When we think about our journey here, the path traced in the previous chapters is illuminated by a sequence of beacons – from burning passion to warm empathy, from authentic communication to unyielding integrity. Each of these elements contributed to the vibrant, multifaceted tapestry of Inspirational Leadership.

Just like a river, which, even in the face of mountains and valleys, always finds its way, continually sculpting the landscape and adapting to the terrain, Inspirational Leadership is fluid, adaptable, and relentless in its pursuit of excellence. The growth mindset is what fuels this current, ensuring that the leader continues to flow, even when faced with seemingly insurmountable obstacles.

Think of a thoughtful farmer who, year after year, cultivates his land. With each season, he learns something new. Some years, an unexpected frost can ruin your harvest, while in others, an unexpected abundance brings joy. But regardless of the challenges and triumphs, the gardener persists, learning, adapting, and growing. Similarly, an inspirational leader with a growth mindset sees every challenge and triumph as an opportunity to learn and grow.

The previous chapters laid the groundwork, establishing the structure of leadership. Now, with the growth mindset, we have the magic ingredient that permeates and brings this structure to life, ensuring that it is not only solid but also alive, vibrant, and constantly evolving.

To conclude, let us remember the well-known metaphor of bamboo. During the first four years, it grows only a few inches above the ground. But by the fifth year, the bamboo shoots up, growing up to thirty meters in just six weeks. What were you doing during those four years? It was growing its roots. Likewise, even when it seems that we are not moving forward, if we maintain our growth mindset, we will actually be strengthening our roots, preparing us for the explosive growth that is to come.

May the continuous journey of learning and growth, so well encapsulated by the growth mindset, be the beacon that illuminates your leadership journey. And may each challenge and triumph serve as a reminder that, in the theater of Inspirational Leadership, growth is not just an act, but another fundamental part of the entire production.

Schematized summary of the chapter

1. Key Concept: Growth Mindset

- **What it is:** The belief that skills and capabilities can be developed through effort and dedication, rather than being fixed and innate.
- **Why it matters:** A growth mindset allows leaders and teams to face challenges as opportunities for learning and evolution, rather than insurmountable obstacles.
- **Practical example:** A leader who, after a failed project, instead of blaming the team, seeks to understand what went wrong and how to improve in the future.

2. Key elements

- **Continuous learning:** The constant search for knowledge and the development of new skills.
- **Resilience:** The ability to overcome obstacles and learn from mistakes.
- **Adaptability:** The ability to adjust to change and new situations.
- **Positivity:** An optimistic outlook on the future and the ability to see opportunities in challenges.

3. Implications and Applications

- **Leadership:** Leaders with a growth mindset inspire their teams to strive for excellence and innovation.
- **Organizational Culture:** The growth mindset creates a work environment where learning and development are valued.
- **Personal development:** Leaders with a growth mindset are always looking to improve themselves and reach new heights.
- **Innovation:** The growth mindset encourages experimentation and the search for new solutions.

4. Conclusion

The growth mindset is one of the pillars of Inspirational Leadership. By adopting this mindset, leaders not only inspire their teams but also create an environment where innovation and success are continuous. The leadership journey is a journey of constant learning, and the growth mindset is the fuel that drives this learning.

Keywords: growth mindset, leadership, learning, development, resilience, innovation, organizational culture.

Call to Action: Leaders, cultivate the growth mindset in yourself and your teams. Embrace challenges as learning opportunities and inspire their employees to do the same. The journey of growth is continuous, and every step you take brings you closer to your full potential.

To reflect

- How can the growth mindset impact how you deal with failures and challenges in your leadership? Reflect on how adopting a growth mindset turns failures into opportunities for learning and innovation.

- What practices can you implement in your team to cultivate a collective growth mindset? Explore practical ways to foster an environment where continuous learning and resilience are encouraged.

- Why is it important to value the growth process and not just the results in your team? Highlight the importance of recognizing and celebrating effort and learning along the journey, strengthening team engagement and motivation.

- How can you use feedback to reinforce the growth mindset in your employees? Encourage the use of feedback as a tool to support the ongoing development of team members, focusing on effort, strategy, and adaptation.

- How can the example of historical leaders who have adopted a growth mindset inspire your daily actions as a leader? Connect growth mindset theory with practical examples of leadership, inspiring actions that promote personal and team growth.

Learn more

DWECK, Carol S. *Mindset: The New Psychology of Success*. Rio de Janeiro: Objetiva, 2017.

9

RESILIENCE AND RECOVERY

Success is not final, failure is not fatal: it is the courage to continue that counts.
- Winston Churchill

At the heart of Inspirational Leadership lies an invaluable and powerful attribute: resilience. Books such as "Option B: Facing Adversity, Building Resilience, and Finding Joy" by Sheryl Sandberg and Adam Grant, and "What They Didn't Tell Me: How to Be a Resilient Leader and Build Teams You Can Trust" by Rajeev Peshawaria brilliantly illuminate this concept, offering deep and practical insights into how leaders can face, learn from, and grow from challenges. In this chapter, we will explore how leaders can strengthen their own resilience while simultaneously inspiring their teams to persist and bounce back, even in the most challenging circumstances.

Resilience, as explored in both books, transcends the idea of simply "hanging in there." It is a dance between accepting reality and having the courage to move forward, facing adversity with a proactive and positive attitude. Resilient leaders see challenges not as insurmountable barriers, but as stepping stones to greater understanding and growth.

Understanding that resilience is not an innate trait, but a developed skill, is crucial. In "What They Didn't Tell Me", Peshawaria highlights the importance of self-leadership and self-knowledge in building resilience. This offers hope and power, as it indicates that we can all learn to be more resilient. The key lies in the way we perceive and react to adversity.

Developing resilience involves cultivating cognitive flexibility. Peshawaria emphasizes the importance of leading with a clear purpose and maintaining an unwavering vision, even in the face of setbacks. As a leader, this also entails encouraging and valuing flexibility and adaptability in the team.

In the context of the teachings of "Option B" and "What They Didn't Tell Me," building communities of care and implementing support networks emerge as crucial aspects in leadership. This approach goes beyond the simple idea of professional support, delving into the depths of human relationships within the work environment. For leaders, this means going beyond conventional responsibilities and taking an active role in creating an environment where the team can openly share challenges and vulnerabilities. This environment fosters not only mutual support but also a culture of collaborative learning that is key to strengthening the resilience of all team members.

An effective practice in this regard is the organization of support circles and decompression sessions. These are informal meetings where team members can open up and share feelings and experiences in a safe and welcoming space. For example, after an intense week, a leader can invite the team to a meeting, either virtual or in-person, creating a space for dialogue and sharing. On these occasions, team members not only have the opportunity to express concerns and challenges, but also to offer and receive support from each other.

Additionally, internal mentorship programs can be extremely beneficial. In these programs, more experienced team members mentor younger ones, providing a valuable source of knowledge and support. In parallel, supportive partnerships between colleagues at similar levels foster a sense of camaraderie and mutual support. These partnerships and mentorship aren't just support networks; They create stronger bonds within the team and foster a culture of continuous learning and personal development.

Another relevant initiative is the holding of workshops focused on interpersonal skills, such as effective communication, conflict management, and emotional intelligence. These workshops help the team acquire the tools they need to deal with both internal and external challenges. They serve to demonstrate the leader's commitment to the growth and development of each team member, in addition to reinforcing the idea that the organization values and invests in the well-being of its employees.

It is essential to establish an environment where *feedback* is an integral part of the organizational culture. That is, creating a space in which feedback is given and received in a constructive and respectful way strengthens communication, mutual respect, and trust within the team. This not only helps with conflict resolution and continuous improvement, but also reinforces a culture where everyone feels valued and heard.

In the leadership journey, challenges are more than mere obstacles; They are crucial opportunities to learn, grow, and innovate. Every adversity faced in the workplace, no matter how intimidating it may seem, carries with it the seed of growth and development. Recovery and growth after these adversities require leaders to think deeply and honestly assess not only their current position but also their future aspirations. This process often entails resetting goals, reviewing strategies, and, crucially, taking time to process and learn from what happened.

Let's consider a hypothetical situation: imagine a team that faced a major setback on an important project. Perhaps a customer gave up at the last minute, or a critical error was discovered. Instead of giving in to frustration or despair, a resilient leader would see this situation as an opportunity for the team to grow. This leader could bring the team together for a *brainstorming* session in which everyone is encouraged to share their views on what went wrong, what could be done differently, and how to avoid such mistakes in the future. Through this collaborative and reflective approach, the team not only learns from the setback but also develops stronger and more innovative strategies for future projects.

Another example can be found in the development of new products. Often, initial failures in the development of a product are critical to its eventual success. An inspirational leader would use these failures as learning opportunities, encouraging the team to analyze and adapt the product design or strategy. This "fail fast and learn fast" mentality can lead to significant innovations and a much stronger product.

Additionally, recovering from adversity in the workplace can mean investing time for self-development and personal growth. For example, a leader who has faced harsh criticism about their management style can use this experience as a catalyst for personal development, perhaps by attending workshops on leadership or seeking feedback and advice from trusted mentors. This commitment to self-development not only benefits the individual leader but also serves as a positive role model for the team, demonstrating that continuous growth and adaptation are valued and necessary for success.

Leaders who embrace challenges as opportunities for learning and growth not only strengthen their own resilience but also inspire their teams to do the same. By redefining goals, reviewing strategies, and reflecting on adversity, they foster a culture of innovation, adaptability, and continuous improvement. Ultimately, it is this ability to learn from difficulties and emerge stronger that defines truly inspiring and resilient leadership.

The way a leader deals with adversity not only shapes their own leadership trajectory, but also sets a standard for the team. When a leader faces challenges, learns from them, and emerges stronger, it acts as a source of inspiration for everyone around them. Transparency about struggles and lessons learned is crucial, as it humanizes the leader figure and encourages team members to take a similar approach in the face of their own difficulties. This transparency is an invitation to empathy and sharing, creating a work environment in which challenges are seen as normal stages of the growth process.

For example, a leader who openly shares about a project that didn't have the expected outcome, but emphasizes the valuable lessons learned during the process, is not only validating the experience of failure, but also encouraging a growth mindset in the team. This can be reflected in how the team approaches new projects, with a more open willingness to experiment and a higher tolerance for risk.

Continuous growth is a key aspect of resilience, and leaders must actively promote continuous development in their teams. This can be achieved by encouraging participation in courses, workshops, and mentorship programs, or by simply promoting reading and research. For example, a leader can create a book club within the team, focusing on literature that promotes leadership skills and personal development, or they can allocate regular time for the team to attend relevant webinars and training. These initiatives not only enhance individual skills but also strengthen the cohesion and resilience of the group as a whole.

In addition, the recognition and celebration of resilience are essential to create an organizational culture in which perseverance and overcoming are valued. This can be done in a variety of ways, such as highlighting team members' achievements in meetings, newsletters, or through token awards. For example, a leader might institute a monthly "Resilience Award," recognizing a team member who has demonstrated an exceptional ability to overcome challenges. These actions not only value individual efforts but also serve as motivation for the entire team to continue facing challenges with courage and determination.

Leaders who exemplify resilience, promote continuous development, and recognize their team's efforts are not only strengthening individual resilience but also cultivating a team that is resilient, adaptable, and ready to meet any challenges that may arise.

In a world filled with unpredictable challenges and constant change, resilience emerges as one of the most crucial qualities for an inspirational leader. But as leaders, how can we cultivate and strengthen this essential skill? The answer lies in a series of mindful actions and practices that not only increase our ability to face adversity, but also allow us to inspire and support our team.

1. **Recognize and Accept Reality**: The first step to resilience is to face the reality of the situation, no matter how difficult it may be. Accepting that challenges and adversity are inevitable parts of life and leadership is key.

2. **Maintain a Positive Outlook**: Cultivate optimism, but remain realistic. View challenges as opportunities for learning and growth, not just obstacles.

3. **Develop Cognitive Flexibility**: Be open to different viewpoints and approaches. The ability to adapt to new information and change your action plan when necessary is a crucial part of resilience.

4. **Build Support Networks**: Create and maintain a robust support network. Strong relationships, both inside and outside the organization, can provide emotional and practical support.

5. **Promote Physical and Mental Well-Being**: Maintain a healthy work-life balance. Resilience is fueled by physical and mental well-being.

6. **Learn from Experiences**: Analyze past failures and challenges to draw valuable lessons. This not only strengthens resilience but also helps to avoid repeating the same mistakes.

7. **Practice Gratitude**: Cultivate an attitude of gratitude. Recognizing and appreciating what you have can transform your perspective and help you cope with adverse situations.

8. **Develop Problem-Solving Skills**: Resilience is often tested in how we face and solve problems. Perfecting critical thinking and problem-solving skills is essential.

9. **Keep Your Purpose in Focus**: Constantly remind yourself of the "why" behind your work. A sense of purpose is a powerful motivator and source of resilience.

10. **Invest in Personal and Professional Development**: Encourage and participate in learning and development

opportunities. Continuous growth is the foundation of resilience.

11. **Celebrate Small Victories**: In times of hardship, recognizing and celebrating small achievements can boost morale and bolster resilience.

12. **Foster a Supportive Team Environment**: Create an environment where failure is seen as part of the learning process. Encourage your team to share challenges and support each other.

13. **Be Proactive in Stress Management**: Implement and practice stress reduction strategies, such as meditation, exercise, or hobbies, to maintain an emotional balance.

14. **Exercise Empathy**: Try to understand and connect with the experiences and feelings of others. Empathy strengthens relationships and creates a more resilient environment.

15. **Reflect Regularly**: Take time to reflect on your experiences, emotions, and reactions. Self-analysis can provide valuable *insights* and strengthen your ability to cope with future adversity.

Resilience is an ongoing journey, and every step taken strengthens not only the leader, but the entire team. As leaders, we have a responsibility to model resilience and create an environment in which it can flourish. By incorporating these actions into our leadership, we will not only be improving our own ability to face adversity, but also inspiring and empowering those around us to do the same.

Leadership Map

Forging the Path to Enduring Leadership

Resilience is like a complex and beautiful dance. It involves movement, adaptation, continuous learning, and most of all, the ability to stand tall, no matter how strong the wind. As an inspirational leader, you are both the dancer and the choreographer of this dance. Your task is to not only master the art of staying resilient but also to guide your team through the steps, teaching them how to dance along with life's adversities.

Remember, true resilience is not about never falling, but rather about how you get up each time you fall. And in every lift, in every recovery step, there is an opportunity to grow, learn, and become a stronger version of yourself and, by extension, strengthen your team. This is the essence of resilient leadership – a leadership that not only weathers storms, but also learns to dance in the rain.

By interweaving the learnings from the preceding chapters with the resilience strategies discussed in this segment, an integral picture of Inspirational Leadership is outlined. This approach can be likened to the meticulous craft of working on a complex tapestry, in which each strand symbolizes a distinct component – purpose, passion, communication, empathy, growth. Resilience, in this context, acts as the unifying element, intertwining all these aspects into a harmonious and robust whole.

In mythology, Ariadne gives Theseus a thread to help him find his way back after entering the labyrinth to face the Minotaur. Here, resilience is described as a "thread" that leaders can offer their teams.

The idea is that, just as Ariadne's thread helped Theseus navigate the maze and overcome a major challenge, resilience can help teams face and overcome adversity in the workplace or in other contexts. Resilience is seen as a crucial tool for turning challenges into opportunities for growth and success. This metaphor suggests that resilience is essential to leading effectively through difficult times, helping people find a way through tricky or challenging situations.

Resilience becomes the primary tool for converting obstacles into stepping stones to development and success.

Throughout the leadership trajectory, each challenge faced can be visualized as a knot in the intricate tapestry of our professional experience. While some knots may initially seem complex and intractable, each of them contributes to the strength and character of the product. Resilience empowers us to approach these knots with patience, acumen, and conviction that we can ultimately use them for the sake of team and leader growth.

In any case, it is crucial to recognize that the core of resilience transcends mere resilience; it encompasses the ability to prosper. Resilience manifests itself in the ability to face challenges not as terminals, but as the beginning of new journeys full of discoveries and possibilities.

In the context of everyday life, resilience can be observed in simple elements, such as the plant that emerges through the fissure in the asphalt, the river that persistently carves its way into the landscape, or the perseverance of the athlete that rises after each fall. Similarly, in leadership, resilience is revealed in the ability to maintain serenity in the midst of adversity, to generate creative solutions in chaotic situations, and to instill hope in adverse circumstances.

I invite you to visualize your own leadership trajectory as a rich and complex tapestry. Each challenge overcome, each triumph achieved, each lesson assimilated weaves this tapestry. Resilience, in this panorama, is the shine that permeates the entire fabric, the characteristic that gives the tapestry not only aesthetic beauty, but also intrinsic firmness and value.

As we move forward, let us take with us the understanding that in the leadership journey, resilience is the thread that leads us through the uncertain, that empowers us to weave a narrative of success and meaning, not only for ourselves, but for all those who share our journey.

Schematized summary of the chapter

1. Main Concept: Resilience in Leadership

- **What it is:** Resilience is the ability to adapt positively to adverse situations, to overcome obstacles, and to recover from difficulties.
- **Why it matters:** Resilient leaders inspire their teams, overcome crises, and build stronger organizations.
- **Practical example:** A leader who, after losing a large client, reorganizes the team, seeks new opportunities and emerges from the crisis with a renewed strategy.

2. Key elements

- **Self-knowledge:** Understanding your own strengths, weaknesses, and reactions to challenging situations.

- **Flexibility:** Ability to adapt to changes and new situations.
- **Optimism:** Maintaining a positive outlook, even in the face of challenges.
- **Building support networks:** Cultivating strong relationships with peers, mentors, and friends.
- **Continuous learning:** Learning from experiences, both positive and negative.

3. Implications and Applications

- **Leadership:** Resilient leaders inspire confidence and motivate their teams, even during difficult times.
- **Organizational culture:** A leader's resilience contributes to the creation of a strong and adaptable organizational culture.
- **Crisis management:** Resilient leaders are more effective at dealing with crises and uncertainty.
- **Well-being:** Resilience is linked to the mental and emotional well-being of leaders and their teams.

4. Conclusion

Resilience is one of the pillars of inspiring leadership. By cultivating resilience, leaders not only overcome challenges but also inspire their teams to do the same. Resilience is a continuous journey that requires self-knowledge, skill development, and the construction of a supportive environment. By embracing resilience, leaders can build stronger, more resilient organizations that are able to meet any challenge.

Keywords: resilience, leadership, adversity, adaptability, growth, organizational culture, well-being.

Call to Action: Leaders, invest in building your resilience and creating a work environment that fosters resilience across the team. By doing so, you will be equipped to face any challenge and build a stronger, more prosperous future.

To reflect

- How can resilience be developed in a leader, and why is it important that this skill is practiced and encouraged within a team? Assess the understanding of resilience as a learned skill and the importance of its application in the context of leadership.

- How can a leader transform adversity into growth opportunities for himself and his team? Explore the leader's ability to turn challenging situations into learning and development experiences.

- What is the role of support networks and care communities in building a culture of resilience within an organization? Analyze the importance of mutual support and creating safe environments to strengthen collective resilience.

- What are the main strategies that a leader can use to foster cognitive flexibility in their team? Assess the leader's ability to promote adaptability and openness to new ideas and approaches among team members.

- How can the recognition and celebration of individual and collective achievements contribute to strengthening resilience within a team? Explore the importance of recognition practices and how they impact team morale, motivation, and resilience.

Learn more

SANDBERG, Sheryl; GRANT, Adam. Option B: Facing Adversity, Building Resilience, and Finding Joy. São Paulo: Companhia das Letras, 2017.

PESHAWARIA, Rajeev. What They Didn't Tell Me: How to Be a Resilient Leader and Build Teams You Can Trust. New York: Penguin Random House, 2022.

10

Dynamic Delegation

> *The secret to success is knowing how to use people, delegate authority, and get the best out of each one.*
> *- John D. Rockefeller*

Inspirational Leadership goes far beyond simply managing tasks or supervising teams. It involves the ability to inspire, empower, and guide others to reach their full potential. At the heart of this approach is delegation – a key skill that allows leaders to distribute responsibilities in such a way that each team member can grow and develop. Richard Branson, founder of the Virgin Group and one of the most innovative entrepreneurs of our era, exemplifies this practice in his trajectory. In his autobiography *Losing My Virginity*, Branson reveals how delegation is not just a management technique, but a philosophy of life that he has cultivated throughout his career, allowing his business to thrive and his teams to excel.

Richard Branson has always seen delegation as an essential tool for success. From the early days of Virgin Records, he understood that in order to grow his business and turn his ideas into reality, he would need to trust the people around him. Delegating, for Branson, is not just about lightening his workload, but about creating a culture of innovation and autonomy. He realized that by giving his employees space to take responsibility, he was not only strengthening the company, but also promoting the individual growth of each team member. By delegating tasks and responsibilities, leaders not only lighten their own workload but also cultivate leaders within their teams. Just as Jesus sent his disciples to preach the gospel, delegating authority to them (Mark 6:7), modern leaders can delegate tasks for their employees to grow and contribute significantly to the success of the organization.

However, delegating is not a simple task. Many leaders, especially those who are highly skilled and have a strong sense of responsibility, may find it difficult to relinquish control. Branson acknowledges this tendency, but argues that true inspirational leadership requires trusting the abilities and judgment of others. It teaches that effective delegation starts with hiring the right people – individuals who share the company's vision and values and who have the autonomy to make independent decisions.

Trust: The Foundation of Delegation

Trust is the foundation on which delegation must be built. Without trust, delegation becomes a simple transfer of tasks, without the real empowerment of employees. Branson has always defended the idea that by trusting their team, a leader creates an environment in which people feel valued and motivated to give their best. He argues that for delegation to be effective, it is necessary for leaders to not only trust the capabilities of their subordinates, but also allow them to learn from their mistakes.

Peter Drucker, one of the most influential thinkers in modern management, reinforces this view when he states: "The most important thing in communication is to listen to what is not being said." For Drucker, effective delegation requires leaders to listen to and understand their teams, trusting them to make the best decisions, even without direct guidance. This mutual trust is what allows delegation to function dynamically and effectively, fostering innovation and growth within the organization.

Delegating doesn't simply mean passing tasks to others. For delegation to be truly effective, it is essential that each delegated task has a clear purpose and is aligned with the organization's strategic objectives. Branson highlights the importance of delegating in a way that challenges and develops the team. He always encouraged his managers to delegate tasks that would provide learning and growth to their subordinates.

John C. Maxwell, a renowned author and leadership expert, states, "A leader is one who knows the way, walks the way, and shows the way." Maxwell emphasizes that while a leader should be an example to follow, it is equally important that they delegate responsibilities so that others can learn and grow. He believes that delegation is essential for the development of future leaders and that without it, an organization cannot truly thrive.

Branson exemplifies this approach on several occasions throughout his career. A powerful example of this is the creation of Virgin Atlantic Airways. When Branson decided to enter the aviation industry, he knew he was sailing into uncharted waters. Instead of trying to master every aspect of the business, he hired industry experts and gave them the autonomy they needed to build the airline. This trust allowed Virgin Atlantic to stand out in the market by offering customer service that was innovative and defied industry conventions.

Empowering the Team

One of the biggest benefits of effective delegation is team empowerment. When a leader trusts their employees and gives them the responsibility of making decisions, they not only lighten their own workload but also motivate team members to take ownership of their tasks. Richard Branson has always encouraged his employees to make decisions and take risks, aware that this attitude is essential for growth and innovation.

Stephen Covey, author of *The 7 Habits of Highly Effective People*, points out that "Delegating effectively to your circle of influence strengthens both the individual and the organization." Covey believes that delegation is not just about allocating tasks, but about widening a leader's circle of influence. When a leader delegates, they strengthen their team, empowering them to take on greater responsibilities while expanding their own leadership skills.

Effective delegation thus becomes a means by which a leader turns a vision into action. It is more than a management mechanism; It is an expression of confidence. A leader who delegates effectively not only distributes tasks but also empowers their employees by offering them the opportunity to grow and contribute meaningfully to the organization's goals. This creates a space in which team members not only see a clear path to personal and professional development, but also feel that their contributions are valued and essential to collective success.

Empowering the team goes beyond simply delegating tasks; it's about making sure team members feel like they have the support and resources they need to succeed. When people feel empowered, they are more inclined to innovate and find creative solutions to problems. This sense of appreciation is a powerful motivator, creating a culture of loyalty and high performance.

We can see that delegating effectively is an *art that every inspirational leader must master*. It's more than simply distributing tasks; It's an act of empowering your team by entrusting them with meaningful responsibilities that foster personal and professional growth. To improve their delegation skills, a leader must adopt a systematic and conscious approach, following strategic steps that ensure both operational effectiveness and the development of their subordinates.

Here are some practical actions inspiring leaders can take to improve their ability to delegate effectively:

1. **Set Clear Objectives:** Before delegating any tasks, it is crucial to define what is expected to be achieved. This not only establishes a parameter of success for the task, but also ensures that everyone involved understands the purpose and importance of their contributions. For example, a project leader at a technology company may need to delegate the development of new software. Before delegating, the leader should clearly define the objectives, such as "Develop a *user-friendly app* that improves the checkout process for customers by the end of the quarter." This clear objective not only guides the team on what needs to be done, but also highlights the importance of the project to the customer experience.

2. **Choose the Right People:** Delegation should be aligned with the skills and passions of the team members. This

means identifying individual skills and delegating tasks that not only challenge employees but are also aligned with their interests and career goals. Considering the same task, the leader should evaluate the skills of each member of the development team. Delegating the *front-end* task to a developer who has passion and experience in creating intuitive interfaces and the *back-end* task to a professional specialized in data security, ensures not only effectiveness, but also the satisfaction and professional development of those involved.

3. **Provide the Necessary Resources:** For delegation to be effective, leaders must ensure that their teams have access to the necessary resources to accomplish the tasks. This includes information, tools, time, and support. In the software development scenario, the leader must ensure that the team has access to software development tools, servers for testing, and enough time to perform quality work. This can also include training on new technologies or methodologies, if necessary.

4. **Communicate Expectations:** Clear communication about expectations is key. This involves explaining the success criteria, deadlines, and desired standards, as well as any other relevant details that may influence performance. Clear communication can be exemplified by the same leader who holds regular meetings to discuss project progress, sets *clear milestones, and makes project documents available that detail technical specifications and expected quality standards.*

5. **Empower, Not Micromanage:** Delegating also means trusting. Leaders should avoid the temptation to micromanage, allowing team members the freedom to approach tasks in a way they deem most effective, within

established standards. Rather than requiring detailed daily updates, the leader can request weekly summaries and be available for discussions or to troubleshoot issues as they arise.

6. **Foster Development:** Delegating can be an excellent opportunity to develop skills in team members. This can be achieved by encouraging continuous learning and offering constructive feedback that helps in professional evolution. Thus, delegating challenging tasks that allow team members to apply and expand their skills is crucial. This can be seen when a leader delegates the responsibility of presenting a project to a team member who wants to develop presentation and communication skills.

7. **Monitor Progress and Be Available:** While micromanagement should be avoided, tracking progress and being available for support and guidance is essential. This helps ensure that tasks are on track and provides a security for employees to feel supported. The leader should establish periodic check-ins to assess progress and adjust directions without suffocating the team with excessive supervision. This helps keep the project on track and demonstrates to team members that the leader is invested in the success of the project and available to help.

8. **Recognize and Celebrate Successes:** A vital aspect of effective delegation is recognizing and celebrating successes. This not only motivates the team but also reinforces the importance of each contribution to the overall success of the organization. When the team meets or exceeds expectations, such as in the successful launch of the software, the leader must recognize and celebrate this success. This can be through a thank you email, a mention at a company meeting, or even bonuses.

9. **Learn from Experience:** Every delegation experience is a learning opportunity. Reflecting on what worked and what didn't can help refine delegation techniques for future initiatives. After a task is completed, it is helpful to conduct a post-project review to discuss what worked well and what could be improved. This may involve gathering feedback from everyone involved and adapting delegation practices based on that information.

By implementing these actions, leaders not only improve their delegation skills but also foster a more dynamic, motivating, and productive work environment. Delegation then becomes not only a management tool, but a leadership tool that fosters continuous growth, innovation and excellence throughout the organization.

The Delegation as a Legacy of Leadership

Effective delegation is not an isolated practice; It is the manifestation of the fundamental principles that shape exemplary leadership, as discussed in the previous chapters of this book. Each aspect of delegation is intrinsically linked to the core values that a leader wants to promote within their team, making it a vital tool for the achievement of organizational objectives.

In Chapter 2, Vision with Purpose, we learned that delegation begins with a clear vision. An effective leader is not limited to distributing tasks; It communicates the 'why' behind each mission. This deep understanding of purpose not only clarifies the 'what' and 'how', but also strengthens the team's commitment and motivation. When team members understand the purpose of their responsibilities, they see beyond daily tasks and connect with the organization's broader goals, which enhances their engagement and dedication.

In *Chapter 3, Passion in Action*, we discussed how the leader's passion can be a powerful catalyst. By delegating, the leader has the opportunity to align tasks with the individual passions of team members, creating a synergy that maximizes both effectiveness and job satisfaction. Delegation then becomes a means of infusing passion, allowing each employee to contribute in a way that resonates with their own interests and aspirations, elevating personal performance and fulfillment.

Chapter 4, Non-Negotiable Integrity, addresses the importance of delegating with integrity. This means providing the necessary resources to carry out tasks, setting clear expectations, and maintaining honest and open communication. Integrity in delegation also involves the responsibility to track progress and offer constructive feedback, ensuring that the team not only understands the goals but also feels supported on their way to achieving them.

Finally, Chapter 5, The Art of Communication, highlights the need for effective communication in delegation. Communicating is not just a process of transmitting information; It is also an exercise in active listening and adaptation to the needs and feedback of the team. Effective delegation uses communication to ensure that everyone on the team understands their responsibilities and how their roles fit into the bigger picture of the organizational vision.

Therefore, delegation should be understood as a natural extension of the principles that each leader must cultivate. It is an act of trust that empowers team members, encouraging them to take on greater responsibilities and develop their skills, while strengthening team cohesion and strategic alignment. By applying these principles, a leader not only delegates tasks but also delegates the opportunity for growth and success, making delegation a powerful tool for achieving organizational excellence.

Dynamic delegation is an art that requires trust, clarity, and a genuine commitment to team development. As Richard Branson demonstrates, when done correctly, delegation not only improves efficiency and productivity, but also strengthens the team, creating an environment where everyone feels empowered and valued. Leading is not about doing everything yourself, but rather about inspiring others to achieve collective success. By delegating effectively, leaders not only multiply their capabilities but also build stronger, more cohesive, and innovative teams.

Indra Nooyi, legendary CEO of PepsiCo, summed up the power of delegation well when he said:

> As a leader, you must learn to delegate with confidence. It's not just about distributing tasks, but about empowering your team to make decisions, trust their abilities, and allow them to grow. This not only lightens their workload, but also develops the next generation of leaders.

The practice of dynamic delegation, as exemplified by Branson and other great leaders, is essential for any leader who wants to not only manage but truly inspire and transform their team and organization. It is a powerful tool for developing inspiring and effective leadership that empowers others to reach their full potential.

Schematized summary of the chapter

1. Main Concept: Dynamic Delegation

- **What it is:** Dynamic delegation is the practice of assigning responsibilities and authority to team members in a strategic way, allowing them to grow and contribute in a meaningful way to the success of the organization.

- **Why it matters:** Dynamic delegation allows leaders to free up time to focus on strategic tasks, empowers team members, and creates a more collaborative and innovative work environment.

- **Practical example:** A CEO delegating to a product manager the responsibility of launching a new product, providing the necessary resources, and tracking progress.

2. Key elements

- **Trust:** The foundation of effective delegation is trust in team members.

- **Clarity:** It is essential to clearly define the responsibilities, expectations, and deadlines for each delegated task.

- **Empowerment:** Delegation involves granting team members authority and autonomy to make decisions.

- **Development:** Delegation should be used as a tool to develop employees' skills and potential.

- **Communication:** Open and transparent communication is essential to ensure that everyone understands their responsibilities and to provide constructive feedback.

3. Implications and Applications

- **Leadership:** Dynamic delegation allows leaders to focus on strategic tasks and develop their teams.

- **Organizational culture:** Effective delegation contributes to the creation of a culture of trust, autonomy, and innovation.

- **Employee engagement:** When employees feel empowered and accountable, they tend to be more engaged and motivated.

- **Team success:** Delegation allows teams to work more efficiently and productively.

4. Conclusion

Dynamic delegation is an essential skill for inspirational leaders. By delegating tasks effectively, leaders not only lighten their own workload, but also empower their employees, foster growth and innovation, and build stronger, more engaged teams. Delegation is not just a management tool, but a leadership philosophy that puts people's trust and development first.

Keywords: delegation, leadership, empowerment, trust, development, team, autonomy, innovation.

Call to Action: Leaders, invest in developing your delegation skills. By delegating tasks effectively, you'll not only free up time to focus on strategic tasks, but you'll also create a more collaborative and productive work environment where your employees can reach their full potential.

To reflect

- To what extent do I trust my team to take responsibility and make decisions? What are my biggest challenges when delegating tasks? This question encourages the leader to reflect on their own ability to delegate and identify the barriers that may be preventing them from empowering their team.

- How can I ensure that delegated tasks are aligned with the organization's strategic objectives? What metrics can I use to assess the impact of delegation on achieving these objectives? This question helps the leader ensure that delegation is not just a way to distribute tasks, but rather a strategy to achieve organizational objectives more efficiently.

- What development opportunities am I offering my team members through delegation? How can I ensure that delegated tasks are challenging enough to promote professional growth? This question encourages the leader to see delegation as a tool to develop the skills and potential of their employees.

- How can I clearly and effectively communicate the expectations and objectives of each delegated task? What is the best way to provide constructive feedback to my employees? This question highlights the importance of clear communication and constructive feedback in delegation, which are essential elements for team success.

- How can I strike the right balance between empowering team members and providing the support they need to succeed? What are the signs that I'm delegating too much or too little? This question helps the leader find the sweet spot between autonomy and support, ensuring that employees feel empowered while also having access to the necessary resources and guidance.

Learn more

BRANSON, Richard. *Losing my virginity*. 1. ed. São Paulo: Globo Livros, 2011.

DRUCKER, Peter F. *The Essential Drucker: Selections from the Management Works of Peter F. Drucker*. New York: Harper Business, 2001.

MAXWELL, John C. *The 21 Irrefutable Laws of Leadership: Follow Them and People Will Follow You*. Nashville: Thomas Nelson, 2007.

COVEY, Stephen R. *The 7 Habits of Highly Effective People: Powerful Lessons for Personal Transformation*. Rio de Janeiro: BestSeller, 2009.

NOOYI, Indra. *My Life in Full: Work, Family, and Our Future*. New York: Portfolio, 2021.

11

INNOVATION AND INSPIRATION

Empowering people is the path to innovation.
- Steve Jobs

Leading is influencing people to do what you want them to do, because they want to do it.
- Dwight D. Eisenhower

In a world characterized by rapid technological evolution and continuous socioeconomic changes, innovation has become the lifeline for organizational survival and success. Far from being a mere luxury, an organization's ability to reinvent itself and inspire its workforce is now an essential requirement to stay relevant in an increasingly competitive market environment. This chapter is dedicated to exploring how outstanding leaders can develop and nurture a culture that not only embraces innovation, but truly celebrates it and integrates it into daily practices, driving excellence at all levels of the organization.

The focus is placed on how this culture of innovation can be established, sustained, and adapted over time, drawing on the insights of visionaries such as Clayton M. Christensen, known for his seminal work on disruptive innovation, and Tom Kelley and David Kelley, who have revolutionized the way we think about design and creativity in the workplace. These thinkers not only challenged old concepts, but offered frameworks that can be applied to unleash creative potential and lead transformation within organizations.

Christensen, in his study of how the most successful companies can do everything "right" and still lose their leadership position in the market, stresses the importance of being aware of changing consumer demands and emerging technology. He argues that true innovation occurs when companies courageously explore new territory, often at risk of cannibalizing their own established products. The lesson here is clear: leading with a vision of the future and a willingness to embrace the unknown is crucial.

On the other hand, Tom Kelley and David Kelley, in the book "Creative Confidence", discuss how the culture of fear and risk aversion stifle natural creativity and innovation in companies. They advocate an approach where error is seen as an essential part of the learning process and experimentation is encouraged. This leadership paradigm not only empowers individuals to express their most audacious ideas, but it also creates an environment in which those ideas can be tested and improved without the fear of failure.

The introduction to this chapter proposes in-depth research into how leaders can shape environments that not only survive waves of change, but also thrive and lead the forefront of innovation. Guided by the teachings of Christensen and the Kelleys, we will examine practical strategies that can be implemented to foster a culture of continuous and inspiring innovation, ensuring that excellence is not an isolated achievement, but a defining characteristic of the organization.

Clayton M. Christensen, in his influential work "The Innovation Dilemma," articulates a fundamental truth about innovation in business: many organizations fail not because of a lack of resources or technology, but because they fail to recognize and embrace disruptive opportunities. He warns that companies often focus excessively on satisfying the needs of their most demanding customers, thus missing out on new emerging markets that could be exploited with innovative products with lower margins and higher volume. So the real lesson for inspirational leaders is the need to constantly be prepared to challenge the status quo and adopt new perspectives that may seem counterintuitive or even risky at first glance.

This concept of disruptive innovation is exemplified in a remarkable way in the career of Steve Jobs, co-founder of Apple. Jobs not only visualized the potential of technology, but he also deeply intuited what people wanted technology to accomplish, often before they were even aware of those desires. Their approach was not simply based on meeting the needs of consumers in a reactive manner; He sought to anticipate and shape these needs with category-defining products. The launch of the iPhone and iPad are testaments to this approach. These devices not only met existing expectations, but also created paradigms for interacting with technology, cementing Apple's reputation as a leader in innovation.

Jobs's ability to see beyond the existing market and imagine what might be possible has transformed entire industries, from telecommunications to media and entertainment. He understood that innovation is not just about making small improvements to existing products, but about completely reimagining how those products can enrich people's lives. This vision requires a deep empathy for human wants and needs, a trait that all inspirational leaders must cultivate.

In addition, innovation leadership entails creating an environment in which the fear of failure does not stifle creativity and experimentation. Apple's culture, under Jobs' leadership, was famous for encouraging bold thinking and calculated risk-taking. This environment allowed Jobs' team to pursue innovative ideas without the burden of fear of failure, a crucial component of fostering a true culture of innovation.

Therefore, cultivating a culture of innovation within an organization requires more than just brilliant ideas or advanced technology; It requires leaders who can see beyond the horizon, who continually challenge existing norms, and who inspire their teams to do the same. Leaders like Steve Jobs exemplify how the combination of futuristic vision and a deep understanding of human needs can create not only transformative products but also a lasting legacy of innovation and inspiration.

Tom Kelley and David Kelley, in "Creative Confidence," demystify the notion that innovation is exclusively the territory of isolated "creative geniuses." They argue that the ability to innovate is universal and that everyone has creative potential, just waiting to be unlocked. The key, they say, is to cultivate an environment that welcomes new ideas and treats failure as a crucial and instructive step in the learning and innovation process.

One of the best examples of this philosophy in action is Google's culture, which is recognized for its innovative management practices that encourage creativity and experimentation. Google notably allows its employees to use up to 20% of their work time on personal projects that they believe will benefit the company. This policy, known as the "20% Rule," is responsible for the birth of revolutionary products like Gmail, Google News, and

AdSense. The logic behind this policy is simple: when people have the freedom to explore their passions and curiosities, they are more likely to develop innovations that can transform the market.

Effective leaders understand the importance of creating safe spaces for experimentation, in which not only is error allowed, but error is seen as a vital component of the innovation process. These leaders foster a culture in which fear of failure does not stifle creativity and initiative. Instead, each failure is seen as an opportunity for growth and a stepping stone on the road to success.

The Kelleys' approach to accessible and democratized innovation suggests that everyone in the organization, regardless of their job title or function, should be encouraged to think creatively and come up with new ideas. This entails providing training and resources to help employees develop their creative thinking skills and feel confident in their innovation capabilities.

Additionally, an inspirational leader should act as a facilitator, not only supporting new ideas but also ensuring that there are processes and tools available so that those ideas can be tested and implemented. This can include everything from structured brainstorming sessions and innovation workshops to feedback systems that help refine and enhance proposals.

Ultimately, encouraging new ideas is about nurturing a culture of curiosity, openness, and mutual respect, where everyone feels their contributions are valued. Leaders who cultivate these environments not only foster innovation within their teams, but also inspire their employees to achieve higher levels of excellence and job satisfaction. Google's culture and Kelley's philosophy show us that when people feel that their ideas are welcomed and that their work has a purpose, they are more likely to innovate and contribute to the overall success of the organization.

The emotional connection to work is not only a component of personal satisfaction, but also a potent catalyst for innovation and productivity. Notable leaders, such as Nelson Mandela, exemplify how passion and an overarching purpose can bring people and resources together around a unified vision, driving meaningful and lasting change.

Mandela, with his tireless fight for justice and equality, not only led the transformation in South Africa but also served as a source of global inspiration. He showed that the true power of a leader lies in the ability to infuse their own convictions and values into a larger movement, motivating people not only to follow but to take an active part in creating a new reality. His ability to link the mission of the anti-apartheid movement to the individual and collective values of his followers transformed a political struggle into a palpable cause that resonated deeply on a personal level.

Similarly, in the business environment, effective leaders should strive to connect the organization's mission to the personal values of their team members. In doing so, they transform day-to-day operations into components of a larger mission, ensuring that each task contributes to a broader goal. For example, when a leader of a sustainable technology company communicates how each project contributes to broader environmental solutions, they not only inform the team about what is being done, but also why it is important. This can transform employee engagement, as they see their daily work as part of a larger effort to make a difference in the world.

In addition, infusing passion and purpose requires leaders to be transparent about the organization's goals and challenges. This involves opening candid dialogues about where the company is and where it intends to go, allowing team members to see how their individual contributions fit into the bigger picture. This type of leadership not only increases loyalty and commitment, but also fosters an environment where innovation is natural and encouraged.

Leaders who can implement this connection between work and individual values create a space in which motivation is intrinsic. As Simon Sinek points out in "Start with Why," organizations and leaders that operate with a clear sense of purpose not only attract high-caliber talent, but also cultivate a culture of commitment and creativity that is difficult to replicate. These are the organizations that not only respond to change, but lead change by setting new standards and innovating beyond market expectations.

Instilling passion and purpose is therefore critical not only to team motivation but also to an organization's ability to be resilient and innovative in times of change. The lesson of great leaders like Mandela and the advice of thinkers like Simon Sinek teach us that when passion and purpose are aligned, the possibilities are endless and the results can transform not just companies, but entire societies.

Building Resilience and Adaptability

Innovation is a continuous process that extends beyond the mere generation of creative ideas; It requires the ability to persist and adapt in the face of challenges and unforeseen changes. Clayton M. Christensen, in his analysis of disruptive innovation, emphasizes that organizations that thrive are those that not only react to changes with agility but also anticipate and direct them. This perspective is reinforced by Tom Kelley, who emphasizes the importance of flexibility and openness to feedback in leadership, allowing for a constant evolution of organizational strategies.

Resilience and adaptability are therefore essential for any organization that aspires to sustained innovation. For example, Apple, under the leadership of Steve Jobs and later Tim Cook, demonstrated an exceptional ability to adapt and evolve. Not only has the company introduced revolutionary products that have defined market categories, such as the iPhone and iPad, but it has also been able to adapt to changing consumer habits and technological advancements, while remaining at the forefront of the technology industry.

This ability to adapt and resilience is often forged in times of crisis. During the 2008 financial crisis, for example, many companies had to reevaluate and significantly alter their operations and strategies. Those that were able to adapt quickly to the new economic conditions not only survived, but often emerged stronger. Resilience, in this context, is less about resisting change and more about the ability to transform in response to them.

Tom Kelley argues that the key to building this organizational resilience lies not only in the ability to adapt, but also in cultivating a culture that encourages experimentation and continuous learning. This means creating an environment where mistakes are seen as opportunities for growth and where feedback is not only accepted but actively sought.

For example, companies like Google and Amazon have cultures that encourage experimentation and failure. At Google, employees are encouraged to spend a portion of their work time on projects that interest them, even if those projects are not directly related to their roles. This policy helped create innovative products, such as Gmail and Google News, that grew out of employee side projects.

To build a culture that truly embraces innovation, leaders must focus on nurturing resilience and adaptability, incorporating practices that foster flexibility, continuous learning, and a willingness to adjust or change course when necessary. This entails not only leading by example, but also providing the tools and resources that allow teams to explore new ideas and learn from the results, whether success or failure.

In short, an organization's ability to innovate depends deeply on its resilience and adaptability. Leaders who cultivate these qualities in their teams and strategies ensure that their organization not only responds to change, but also anticipates them and uses them as levers for continued growth and innovation.

Becoming an Inspiring Catalyst for Innovation

In today's dynamic business landscape, leaders are not just asset managers; They are the catalysts that inspire innovation and drive transformation within their organizations. To be effective in this role, they must adopt practices that not only generate new ideas, but also cultivate an environment in which those ideas can flourish and turn into innovative solutions. The following are practical actions that leaders can implement to improve their ability to inspire and sustain innovation:

1. **Establish a Clear and Shared Vision**: For an organization to thrive in an ever-changing business landscape, it is crucial for leaders to establish a clear and shared

vision. This vision should be aligned with the company's strategic goals, ensuring that every action and innovation contributes directly to the larger goals. It is essential to communicate this vision in a clear and inspiring way, ensuring that each team member understands their role and how their individual contributions propel the collective towards shared success.

- o Define and communicate a clear vision for innovation that aligns with the company's strategic objectives.
- o Ensure that each team member understands how their work contributes to this vision.

2. **Cultivate an Environment of Openness and Trust**: Creating an environment of openness and trust is equally vital. Encouraging open communication and sharing of ideas in a space where there is no fear of judgment allows creativity to flourish. Developing a culture in which employees feel safe to explore and experiment is the foundation for genuine innovation. In this environment, risks are seen as opportunities for learning and growth.

- o Encourage open communication and sharing ideas without fear of judgment.
- o Build a culture of trust where employees feel safe to explore and experiment.

3. **Promote Diversity of Thought**: Diversity of thought is another key pillar for innovation. Fostering collaboration between different departments and specializations can create a rich tapestry of ideas and perspectives. In addition, recruiting and developing talent from diverse backgrounds not only enriches discussions but also opens the

door to innovative approaches that may not be considered in a homogenous environment.

- Encourage collaboration across departments and specializations to combine different perspectives.
- Recruit and develop talent from diverse backgrounds to enrich discussions and approaches.

4. **Facilitate Access to Resources and Tools**: Innovation also requires organizations to facilitate access to resources and tools necessary for experimentation and rapid prototyping. Offering educational resources and continuous learning opportunities helps keep staff up-to-date with the latest trends and technologies, strengthening their ability to innovate effectively.

    - Provide the tools and technologies needed for experimentation and rapid prototyping.
    - Offer educational resources and learning opportunities to keep your team up-to-date with the latest trends and technologies.

5. **Establish Metrics to Monitor Innovation**: To measure and foster innovation, it is essential to establish clear metrics that reflect progress towards innovation goals. These metrics can help adjust strategies and processes, ensuring that the organization stays on track and adapts as needed.

    - Define and track metrics that reflect progress towards innovation goals.
    - Use these metrics to adjust strategies and processes as needed.

6. **Recognize and Reward Innovative Efforts**: Recognizing and rewarding innovative efforts is crucial for maintaining motivation and enthusiasm for innovation. Implementing recognition systems that value both successes and valid attempts reinforces the culture of innovation and encourages the team to continue striving for excellence.

    - Implement recognition systems that value both successes and valid attempts at innovation.
    - Celebrate the big and small wins to stay motivated and excited for innovation.

7. **Develop Organizational Adaptability**: Organizations must develop an adaptability that allows leaders and teams to respond flexibly to challenges and changes in the market. Fostering a mindset of learning from mistakes turns failures into stepping stones to future success.

    - Train leaders and teams to respond flexibly to challenges and changes in the market.
    - Encourage a "learn from mistake" mindset, where failures are seen as opportunities for growth.

8. **Incorporate Feedback into the Innovation Cycle**: Establishing channels for receiving ongoing feedback from customers, partners, and team members on new initiatives and products helps to ensure that the organization remains relevant and aligned with market needs.

    - Create channels for continuous feedback from customers, partners, and team members on new initiatives and products.
    - Adjust products and strategies based on this feedback to better align with market needs.

9. **Fostering Participatory Leadership**: Promoting participatory leadership can empower team members to take on leadership roles in innovation projects. Allowing teams to manage their own innovative projects within clear guidelines can lead to greater engagement and more meaningful results.

    - Encourage team members to take leadership roles in innovation projects.
    - Promote autonomy by allowing teams to manage their own innovative projects within clear guidelines.

10. **Learning from Other Industries and Cultures**: Fostering exchanges and partnerships with organizations from different sectors is an excellent way to inspire new perspectives and practices.

    - Encourage the exploration of ideas and solutions from other industries that can be adapted or integrated.
    - Promote exchanges and partnerships with organizations from different sectors to inspire new perspectives and practices.

By implementing these actions, leaders can not only improve their delegation skills, but also become true drivers of innovation, inspiring their teams to reach new heights of creativity and excellence. In doing so, they lay the foundation for an organization that not only adapts to the future, but actively shapes it.

Schematized summary of the chapter

1. Main Concept: Culture of Innovation

- **What it is:** An organizational culture that values and encourages the generation of new ideas, experimentation, and adaptation to change.

- **Why it matters:** A culture of innovation is crucial for an organization's survival and growth in a dynamic and competitive market.

- **Practical example:** Google's culture of innovation, which allows employees to dedicate some of their time to personal projects, resulting in revolutionary products like Gmail.

2. Key elements

- **Clear vision:** Leaders must communicate a clear and inspiring vision that drives innovation efforts.

- **Culture of openness:** An environment where new ideas are welcomed and failure is seen as a learning opportunity.

- **Diversity of thought:** The appreciation of different perspectives and experiences to generate more creative ideas.

- **Experimentation:** The creation of a safe environment to test new ideas and learn from the results.

- **Inspiring leadership:** Leaders who motivate and inspire their employees to pursue innovation.

3. Implications and Applications

- **Leadership:** Inspiring leaders create cultures of innovation that drive organizational growth and transformation.

- **People management:** A culture of innovation increases employee engagement and promotes talent development.

- **Strategy:** Innovation is essential for adapting to market changes and developing new products and services.

- **Organizational culture:** A culture of innovation strengthens the organization's identity and makes it more resilient.

4. Conclusion

Innovation is not just an activity, but a culture that needs to be cultivated and nurtured by inspiring leaders. By creating an environment in which creativity is valued, risk is accepted, and learning is continuous, leaders can transform their organizations into true engines of innovation. The journey to innovation is a journey of discovery, adaptation, and continuous growth. By embracing this journey, leaders can inspire their teams to reach new heights of excellence and shape the future.

Keywords: innovation, leadership, organizational culture, creativity, adaptation, vision, purpose, team, development.

Call to Action: Leaders, invest in creating a culture of innovation in your organizations. Encourage curiosity, experimentation and collaboration. By doing so, you will not only be ensuring the survival of your companies, but also contributing to a brighter and more innovative future.

To reflect

- To what extent does my team feel comfortable sharing new and different ideas? What are the barriers that prevent the free expression of innovative ideas in my team? These questions encourage the leader to reflect on the environment they have created and to identify areas where the culture of innovation can be strengthened.

- Is my vision for the organization clear and inspiring to the team? How can I communicate this vision more effectively so that each team member feels connected to a larger purpose? These questions help the leader assess whether their vision is being communicated in a clear and motivating way, and identify opportunities to strengthen that alignment.

- How can I foster diversity of thought within my team? What are the concrete actions I can take to create a more inclusive and responsive environment for different perspectives? These questions encourage the leader to look for ways to create a more diverse and inclusive environment in which innovation can flourish.

- How can I create an environment where experimentation and calculated risk are valued? What are the steps I can take to mitigate the risks associated with innovation? These questions help the leader balance the need for innovation with risk management, creating an environment where experimentation is encouraged in a safe way.

- How can I identify and develop innovative talent within my team? What learning and development opportunities can I provide to stimulate growth and innovation? These questions encourage leaders to invest in the development of their employees, providing them with the tools and support they need to contribute innovative ideas.

Learn more

Christensen, Clayton M. **The Innovation Dilemma.** 1st ed., Harvard Business School Press, 1997.

Kelley, Tom; Kelley, David. **Creative Confidence.** 1st ed., Houghton Mifflin Harcourt Publishing, 2013.

12

WORDS CONVINCE, EXAMPLE DRAGS!

> *Be the change you want to see in the world.*
> *- Mahatma Gandhi*

Leadership by example is, without a doubt, the foundation of all great leadership. The best leaders are not those who only talk about what they believe, but those who demonstrate their beliefs and values through their everyday actions. This truth becomes even clearer when we look at the various aspects of leadership explored in the previous chapters of this book. In each of them, the essence of leadership by example permeates the reflections and practices that were discussed. During my more than 30 years of experience, both in the public sector and in academia, one lesson has become clear to me: to lead is to act. A leader's true influence comes not only from their ability to communicate a vision, but from their ability to live that vision, inspiring their team to follow it genuinely.

Leadership by example finds its roots in the military tradition, where leaders are forged under intense pressure and responsibility. And it was not by chance that I left the topic of leadership by example for this last chapter. My journey in leadership began early, and was forged in the rigor of my military training. As an Army lieutenant, I learned in practice the profound meaning of leading by example. The motto that marked this phase of my life, "words convince, example drags", became a guiding principle that I carry with me to this day. In the military environment, there was no room for empty promises or inspiring speeches without substance. The team followed the leader who was willing to face the same challenges, to deal with difficulties head-on, and to act with integrity in each situation. The trust that soldiers place in their commanders is built on the certainty that the leader will be with them in the most challenging situations.

Historical military leaders, such as Alexander the Great, exemplified this practice. Alexander was known to fight alongside his troops, demonstrating the same courage he expected from his soldiers. This leadership by example engendered loyalty and commitment, motivating his troops to forge ahead, even in the face of nearly impossible challenges. In modern leadership, the same principles apply, whether in high-pressure environments or in routine situations: the leader is the one who guides the team, not just by words, but by actions.

This experience has shown me that example is not just a matter of strategic leadership; it is a culture catalyst. If the leader is the one who makes an effort, who faces adversity with courage and resilience, the team feels this energy and aligns with this attitude.

Throughout my career, this same approach to leading by example has been crucial in all the contexts in which I have worked, regardless of the institutions or positions held. As a leader, I realized that it wasn't enough to just provide guidelines or explain the importance of an initiative to the team. Effective leadership required active participation, especially in the most challenging times. Leadership by example, as John Maxwell taught in his book *"The 21 Irrefutable Laws of Leadership",* is one of the main factors that generates credibility. When team members see the leader willing to face challenges side by side, make difficult decisions, and deal with practical obstacles, trust in leadership increases significantly.

In large projects I learned that leadership by example was the key to keeping the team motivated and focused on results. It was no use just communicating the importance of the project and expecting maximum dedication from the team; It was necessary to be present, face challenges alongside them and actively participate in problem solving. This direct involvement demonstrates commitment, as Jim Collins addresses in *"Companies Built to Win,"* where he describes "Level 5" leadership, which combines personal humility and professional will, the latter being characterized by a willingness to lead with actions.

In academia, as a professor and course coordinator, leadership by example becomes even more evident. When we are in front of students, students observe attitudes more than words. To truly engage them, it was necessary for me to demonstrate the commitment and passion I expected from them. This means being constantly available for debates, investigating new trends and applying innovative methodologies in the teaching process. If I wanted my students to be curious and innovative, as teachers like Paulo Freire in *"Pedagogy of Autonomy"* argue, I needed to be the first to show curiosity, seek new ways of teaching and never settle for old-fashioned methods. This practice was essential for students to realize that learning does not have an end point, but is a continuous journey of growth and discovery.

A clear example of this leadership by example in education happened in a cybersecurity class I taught in college. When introducing new network security software that most students had never used before, I realized that many were intimidated by the complexity of the tool. Instead of waiting for them to master the content themselves, I decided to explore the software together with them, solving problems live during lessons. This not only broke the barrier of fear, but also showed that, even with 30 years of experience, continuous learning is part of a leader's life. As a result, students felt more comfortable trying, making mistakes, and seeking creative solutions to challenges.

Simple actions like these demonstrate that the leader must live the learning and innovation he preaches. This connects directly with the ideas of Simon Sinek, author of *"Leaders Serve Last,"* who talks about the importance of leadership that puts the needs of the team and collective growth above one's own ego. In practice, by demonstrating curiosity, humility, and willingness to continuous learning, the leader creates an environment in which people feel encouraged to give their best, to collaborate, and to be equally curious and innovative.

In the academic landscape, this stance not only engages students but creates a culture of shared responsibility. When students perceive that the teacher is willing to delve deeper with them into the complex issues, they feel that they are part of a collaborative process. And this is fundamental to transform teaching into a rich experience, in which each one feels that they have an active role in the construction of knowledge.

In addition, leading by example does not mean being infallible, but rather being transparent in difficulties. On the times I faced technical or management challenges, I was always open with my team about the obstacles. Instead of hiding flaws or pretending to have all the answers, I showed that being a leader is also being human, being willing to learn and grow from difficulties. This honest approach creates an environment of trust, where the team feels comfortable taking risks and making mistakes, knowing that leadership is there for them, ready to support and refocus when needed.

One of the greatest lessons I learned in my military training and that I take to all aspects of my life is that the example does not drag only because it demonstrates technical ability, but because it demonstrates values. Integrity, courage, resilience, and humility are virtues that need to be lived daily by those who aspire to lead effectively. When these qualities are present in the leader, they become the basis of the organizational culture and inspire everyone around them to seek excellence not only because it is expected, but because it is experienced.

This truth becomes even clearer when we look at the various aspects of leadership explored in the previous chapters of this book. In each of them, the essence of leadership by example permeates the reflections and practices that were discussed.

In Chapter 1, as we demystified the figure of the "perfect leader," we recognized that the most effective leaders are not those who distance themselves through a façade of infallibility, but those who are genuine in their vulnerabilities. When a leader admits his mistakes and acts transparently, he creates an environment of trust, as we saw in the journey of demystifying perfection. Thus, authenticity becomes a fundamental pillar of leadership by example.

Clear vision with purpose, discussed in Chapter 2, is another crucial element for leading by example. It is not enough to set a goal; The true leader is the one who lives this vision with every decision, every action. This commitment inspires everyone around you to dedicate themselves with the same focus and determination. As discussed in the chapters on communication (Chapter 5) and engagement (Chapter 6), the leader who "walks his talk" mobilizes his team not only with words, but with behaviors that mirror what he wants to see in others.

Throughout the previous chapters, we have explored themes such as resilience (Chapter 9), innovation (Chapter 11), and dynamic delegation (Chapter 10). All of these aspects of leadership can only be truly effective when the leader embodies them. A leader who wants to encourage innovation must himself be willing to take risks and embrace new ideas, demonstrating courage and openness to change. Similarly, when we talk about delegation, as discussed in Chapter 10, you need to trust your team, but also be willing to take responsibility, being the first to act when necessary.

Leading by example is an invitation for everyone in the organization to follow the journey of continuous growth, as discussed throughout this book. It is an invitation to live the values we want to see in our teams, to be the change we want to promote and, above all, to transform the work environment into a space where integrity, effort and passion are visible. That is why I continue to reaffirm that leadership by example is, first and foremost, a daily commitment. It is a journey that has no end, as each day offers new opportunities to influence, motivate and transform. May you, the reader, take with you this fundamental lesson: the true leader does not just talk, he acts. And it is through these actions that he inspires, motivates and leaves a lasting legacy.

Thus, I argue that leadership by example is the core of all great leadership. No matter the context, whether in military training, in the public sector or in academia, people follow those who demonstrate commitment, integrity and courage. Leading is not just about giving directions, but about walking together, facing challenges side by side, showing through actions the values that you want to see reflected throughout the team. The example drags because it translates, in a practical and tangible way, what words cannot fully express.

An Inspiring Call to Action

As we come to the end of this last chapter, it is important to recognize that the strategies and insights discussed are not just abstract theories, but rather practical tools designed to trigger a profound transformation in both leaders and the teams they lead. This is a call to action, inviting all leaders, both emerging and established, to leave an indelible mark on their organizations and the world around them.

You, as a leader, possess a unique ability not only to envision the future, but also to inspire those around you to build it with you. This power of influence is similar to that of a gardener, who not only plants seeds, but nourishes each shoot with dedication, until they bloom and bear fruit. Just as the gardener chooses the proper soil, fertilizes and waters with precision, you must cultivate an environment in which new ideas can germinate and thrive. By infusing each project with meaning and purpose, you turn routine tasks into vital pieces of a great mosaic of innovation.

Leading by example, especially in times of change, is like being the captain of a ship in uncharted waters. Just as the captain uses all the navigational tools to find the best course through storms and rough seas, you must guide your crew through challenges, using your vision, passion, and determination to reach new horizons of success and achievement.

An inspirational leader's journey is essentially about turning the impossible into the possible. It's about seeing beyond the limits of the conventional, recognizing that every challenge is an opportunity for innovation and growth. Just as a lighthouse illuminates the stormy seas for ships at night, your leadership should serve as a guiding light, showing the way amidst the obscurity of uncertainty and inspiring your team to keep moving forward, even when the destination seems far away.

End this reading not as the end of a book, but as the beginning of a transformative journey. Let every page you read turn into a step toward leadership excellence. Cultivate a mindset that embraces innovation and celebrates creativity, and see how even the simplest actions can create waves of impact that reverberate far beyond the walls of your organization.

May your leadership be like the water that, gently but with unstoppable force, shapes the stones and alters the landscapes around you. Inspire, motivate and, above all, transform – because it is in your ability to change the world around you that the true essence of inspiring leadership lies.

Schematized summary of the chapter

1. Introduction: Leading by Example

- Leadership by example is the fundamental foundation of all great leadership.
- The best leaders demonstrate their beliefs and values through everyday actions, not just words.
- A leader's true influence comes from their ability to live their vision and inspire their team through their actions.

2. Military Training: Guiding Principles

- Military training in the Army was fundamental in shaping the understanding of leadership by example.
- The motto "words convince, example drags" has become a guiding principle.
- In the military environment, trust was earned through actions, not empty promises or speeches.

3. The Example as a Catalyst for Culture

- The example of the leader defines the organizational culture.
- If the leader faces adversity with courage and resilience, the team aligns with this attitude.
- The leader's energy and dedication drag the team toward the same goals and behaviors.

4. Application in the Professional and Academic Environment

- On large projects and in academia, leading by example involved making difficult decisions alongside the team.
- In the classroom, leading by example was crucial to engaging students and demonstrating a passion for continuous learning.
- The leader must demonstrate curiosity, innovation, and dedication, inspiring others to do the same.

5. Transparency and Humanity: The Basis of Trust

- Leading by example is not being infallible, but being transparent and humane in difficulties.

- Adopting an honest stance, admitting faults, creates an environment of trust and mutual support.
- The leader who recognizes his difficulties and seeks solutions inspires the team to learn and grow from challenges.

6. Core Leadership Values

- Integrity, courage, resilience and humility are virtues that the leader must demonstrate daily.
- These qualities, experienced by the leader, become the basis of the organizational culture, inspiring the team to seek excellence.
- The example defines the patterns and expectations of behavior within the organization.

7. Connection to Previous Chapters

- Chapter 1: Demystifying the "perfect leader" reinforces the importance of a genuine and vulnerable leader.
- Chapter 2: Clear vision with purpose is most effective when lived by the leader in every action and decision.
- Chapters 5 and 6: Effective communication and engagement are maximized when the leader "walks his talk", demonstrating in practice the values he expects to see in the team.
- Chapters 9, 10 and 11: Resilience, dynamic delegation and innovation are only fully effective when the leader exemplifies these values in his or her own actions.

8. Conclusion: An Inspiring Call to Action

- Leading by example is an invitation for everyone in the organization to embark on a journey of continuous growth.
- The true leader acts, lives the values he preaches, inspires and transforms.
- Leadership by example is a daily commitment, which leaves a lasting legacy through actions that impact the lives of others.

9. Metaphors and Reflections

- Leading is like being the captain of a ship, guiding the team through challenges and uncertainty with vision and determination.
- The leader is like a beacon that lights the way for his team, inspiring them to keep going, even in storms.
- Just as a gardener nurtures the growth of plants, the leader sees to it that his team thrives and grows by shaping the environment around him.

10. Finalization

- The example drags because it is a living and tangible expression of the leader's values and vision.
- May each leader recognize the strength of their actions and how they shape the future of their organizations and teams.
- Leading by example is not just a practice; It is the essence of transformative leadership.

Keywords: Leadership by example, Inspiration, Trust, Engagement, Transparency, Authenticity, Resilience, Motivation, Innovation, Transformative action

Call to Action: Want to become a leader who can inspire and motivate your team to reach new heights of success? Discover how leading by example can transform your approach, driving trust, engagement, and lasting results. This book gives you the tools and insights you need to lead with purpose, integrity, and action. Start your journey today to become the leader who turns challenges into opportunities and ideas into achievements!

To reflect

- What is the role of leadership by example in strengthening trust within a team? Explain how active and involved leadership can influence the motivation and performance of team members.

- How did the author's military experience contribute to your view of leadership by example? Describe the fundamental learnings acquired during your training as an Army lieutenant and how it has shaped your approach to leadership.

- Why is it important for a leader to not only communicate a vision, but also to live that vision on a day-to-day basis? Discuss how congruence between speech and action impacts leadership effectiveness and team engagement.

- How does leadership by example manifest itself in the academic environment, according to the author? Report examples given in the chapter on how the author applied leadership by example in the classroom and in course coordination.

- How does transparency in relation to the difficulties faced by the leader influence the team? Analyze the effects of a leader admitting their challenges and mistakes, creating an environment of trust and continuous learning.

Learn more

COLLINS, Jim. **Companies Built to Win**: Why Some Companies Achieve Excellence... and others not. 1. ed. Rio de Janeiro: Campus, 2001.

MAXWELL, John C.. **The 21 irrefutable laws of leadership**: follow them and people will follow you. 1. ed. Rio de Janeiro: Thomas Nelson Brasil, 2007.

SINEK, Simon. **Leaders serve last**: why some teams can come together and others can't. 1. ed. Rio de Janeiro: Sextante, 2014.

ABOUT THE AUTHOR

Fábio Correa Xavier

Fábio Correa Xavier is the Director of the Department of Information Technology (CIO) of the Court of Auditors of the State of São Paulo (TCE-SP) and has more than 30 years of experience in technology and information security. With a Master's degree in Computer Science from the University of São Paulo (USP), Fábio also holds an MBA in Executive Business Management from IBMEC/RJ and a Specialization in Network Engineering from JICA-Japan. His training also includes postgraduate degrees in General Data Protection Law, Public Law, Public Management and Fiscal Responsibility, and Network Projects.

About The Author

Holder of renowned certifications, such as IAPP CIPM (Certified Information Privacy Manager), IAPP CDPO/BR (Certified Data Protection Officer – Brazil), EXIN Privacy & Data Protection and (ISC)² Certified in Cybersecurity, Fábio is recognized for his vast expertise, both in the public and private sectors.

In conjunction with his work at TCE-SP, Fábio is active in the area of pedagogy, being Professor and Coordinator of Undergraduate and Graduate Studies, columnist for MIT Technology Review Brasil and IT Forum, and has more than fifteen years of experience in teaching activities. He is also an evaluator of BASIS courses at MEC/INEP and was a member of the advisory committees of ENADE/2008 and ENADE/2011 in the area of computer networks.

A prominent speaker at several national and international events, Fábio was one of the few Brazilians to participate in the *Microsoft Public Sector Future* podcast and appeared on the cover of *Intelligent CIO LATAM* magazine in August 2024. He is on the list of Top Outstanding Executives in Artificial Intelligence.

Present on the list of Top Outstanding Executives in Artificial Intelligence, he is the author of several reference works in technology, innovation, digitalization and LGPD, Fábio has published the following books:

- *CIO 5.0: The Definitive Guide to Leading Digital Transformation* – Recognized by Exame Magazine as one of the 15 essential books for CIOs, being the only title by a Brazilian author in the selection.
- *LGPD: Good Practices for Brazilian Municipalities*
- *LGPD in the Public Sector: Good Practices for the Adequacy Journey*

- *Cisco Routers: Basic Configuration and Operation Guide*

His career is marked by numerous awards and recognitions, including:

- IT Executive of the Year Award by IT Forum 2023 and 2024
- 2023 Success Case Award at 4CIO Public Sectors
- TOP50 Most Outstanding Executives of the Year 2024 in Artificial Intelligence, by 7th Experience
- IBGP 10 years of Innovation in the Public Sector Award with a focus on the Citizen
- Featured Speaker at ENASTIC MP and TCs, 2023
- Ranking 100 Companies + Innovative in the Use of IT in 2020, 2021 and 2022 (TCESP)
- +Digital Company Award 2020, Government category
- Security Leaders Case of the Year Award
- Minister Gama Filho Award 2019 of the Court of Auditors of the State of Rio de Janeiro
- National Fiscal Education Award 2019 from Febrafite
- IT Executive Honored at 4Network Awards 2019
- Winner of the 2013 Security Leaders Award in the area of Government (finalist in 2014 and 2018)

Even with all these activities, Fábio dedicates part of his time to volunteer work, acting as Executive Secretary of the Technology, Governance and Information Security Management Committee of the Rui Barbosa Institute (IRB) and as a member of the Board of Directors of the Dr. Arnaldo Cancer Institute.

About The Author

Fábio Correa Xavier is also a renowned expert in technology and digital governance, with extensive experience in leading digital transformations in various organizations. Author of several successful books, Fábio stands out for his ability to translate complex concepts into clear and accessible language, making them understandable to a wide audience.

His works, such as "CIO 5.0: The definitive guide to leading digital transformation" and "LGPD: good practices for Brazilian municipalities", have become references in their respective areas, being used by professionals and students from all over the country. Through his works, Fábio contributes significantly to the advancement of the discussion on topics such as innovation, data governance, and digital transformation, inspiring leaders and organizations to build a more digital and sustainable future.

http://www.fabioxavier.com.br/

https://www.linkedin.com/in/fabiocorreaxavier/

https://twitter.com/fabiocx

BOOKS AND CHAPTERS BY THE AUTHOR

CIO 5.0: The Ultimate Guide to Leading Digital Transformation

With valuable insights and a hands-on approach, **CIO 5.0** is your compass for navigating the complex world of ever-evolving technology. Discover how to become a change agent, driving innovation and building a strong digital future for your organization. Covering everything from the latest trends in technology to the best management practices, this book is essential for any CIO looking to transform their company and stand out in the market. Considered one of the best books on technology leadership by Exame Magazine, **CIO 5.0** is your complete reference for digital transformation. Covering everything from the basics of technology to the most advanced trends, this book is indispensable for any professional looking to stand out in the market.

LGPD: good practices for Brazilian municipalities

The work elucidates the contours of the use of information and the impacts brought by the LGPD to the public authorities, bringing a framework of guidelines based on the guidelines prepared by the National Data Protection Authority (ANPD) and good governance practices aimed at public entities, in addition to establishing doctrinal concepts developed by the country's leading privacy and data protection specialists.

LGPD in the Public Sector: Good practices for the adaptation journey

This book presents a collection of articles on the application of the LGPD in the public sector, presenting good practices and recommendations given by the National Data Protection Authority – ANPD, through several informative guides, especially the Guide for Data Processing by the Public Authorities, the Information Security Guide for Small Processing Agents and the Guidance Guide for Definitions of Personal Data Processing Agents and the Person in Charge. The book brings recommendations and good practices for the public sector in general, addressing aspects related to the use of anonymization and pseudonymization techniques, and other relevant topics on privacy and data protection.

Cisco Routers: Basic Configuration and Operation Guide

This book explains, step-by-step, how to set up and operate a Cisco router. It clearly translates concepts and components of routers, comparing them with personal computers, which facilitates understanding and demystifies this very important equipment.
For the most productive reading, this book presents a network scenario providing the reader with the tools (commands and their explanations) necessary to configure it.
This book is intended for students and networking professionals who want to learn how to set up a Cisco router and are entering the fascinating world of networking.

Technology, innovation and other subjects: under analysis

This is a work that brings together the articles, thoughts and analyses that were published in various media during the years 2019 and 2020. In a single work, you will find articles that deal with technology, innovation, human behavior in the IT area, written in a light way and without the intention of becoming a reference, but a source of complementary information for those interested in this exciting area of information technology.

Data Protection Governance Booklet for Municipalities

The General Law for the Protection of Personal Data is already a reality in the Public Administration. Considering the applicability of the LGPD, in order for municipalities to achieve an adequate level of compliance with the guidelines provided for in the Law, it is necessary to implement a data protection culture that corroborates with all spheres and society.

To achieve this goal, the Brazil Governance Network (RGB), together with the Latin American Institute of Governance and Public Compliance (IGCP) and with the support of the National School of Public Administration (ENAP), has just launched a Booklet, which was prepared by the LGPD Committee of the RGB, of which the author is one of the coordinators.

The Courts of Auditors, the pandemic and the future of control

An initiative of the Rui Barbosa Institute and coordinated by Counselor Edilberto Carlos Pontes Lima (TCE-CE), the work aims to bring together reflections on the future of control institutions in the face of institutional experiences with the coronavirus pandemic has the power, first of all, to pay tribute to the direct and indirect victims of this catastrophe.

Fábio Correa Xavier was the author of the chapter entitled "**Minimum steps necessary for the adaptation to the LGPD by the Brazilian Courts of Auditors**".

Comments on the General Law for the Protection of Personal Data

The work "Comments on the General Law for the Protection of Personal Data", by Editora Migalhas, brings together articles by leading experts in the area and addresses actions for adequacy, challenges and solutions.

Fábio Correa Xavier is the author of the chapter **"Actions for adaptation to the LGPD by the Public Administration"**.

www.ingramcontent.com/pod-product-compliance
Lightning Source LLC
Chambersburg PA
CBHW071022240526
45469CB00006BD/2047